بسم الله الرحمن الرحيم

In the Name of Allah, the Most Merciful, the Most Gracious

200+ Ways the Quran Corrects the Bible:
How Islam Unites Judaism and Christianity

Accredited by the Islamic Research Academy of Al Azhar University 2-15-2004

Also by Mohamed Ghounem

101 Bible Quotes on Christ Disproving Trinity

The Apple and the Crucifix: Christianity Revealed

Who is Our Savior? Allah or Jesus

When Christians Ask: The Quran Answers

When Jews Ask: The Quran Answers

When Secularists Ask; The Quran Answers

Leaving Judaism for Islam: Jews Speak Out

Jews and Muslims Agree: From Laws to Love

Why We Die: From Ancient to Modern Philosophies

For More Orders, go to http://www.MuslimPlanet.com

200+ Ways the Quran Corrects the Bible:
How Islam Unites Judaism and Christianity

ISBN: 0-9728518-8-7

Library of Congress Catalog Card Number: 2003115711

Manufactured in the United States of America
Cover Design: Adeel Malik, Brooklyn NY

Multi-National Muslim Committee (MNMC)
PO Box 3491
Newtown CT. 06470 USA

http://www.MuslimPlanet.com

Publisher's Cataloging in Publication

Ghounem, Mohamed
200+ Ways the Quran Corrects the Bible: How Islam Unites Judaism and
Christianity / [Mohamed Ghounem]
1st ed.
p. cm.
Includes bibliographical references and index.
Preassigned LCCN: 2003115711
ISBN: 0-9728518-8-7

1.   Koran --Relation to the Bible.   I. Title.
2.   Islam --Relations --Judaism.   II. Title.
3.   Islam --Relations –Christianity. III. Title.
4.   Apologetics.
BP134.G4 2004

Forward

Love brings people together. In a beautiful and melodious method, the Quran brings harmony between Jews and Christians. Enjoining the scriptures into one, the Quran mediates, reconciles, and unites.

Love comes from mutual understanding and coherent communication. The Quran preserved in its original language and version for nearly 1,400 years, has been a clear untainted light of guidance.

As a growing number of Jews and Christians pose perplexing questions to their Biblicists, the gap is growing between God and humans. Many of these questions have been on the stage of debate between Jews and Christians, causing unbridgeable animosity between the two. The Quran solves these questions, building a bridge of understanding between humans and God.

Seeking to bring peace and agreement among humans, the Quran divinely arbitrates the differences between Jews and Christians, uniting them into Muslims. This volume magnifies some of the miracles of the Quran by demonstrating hundreds of ways the Quran rectifies the Bible:

"To thee We sent the Scripture in truth, confirming the scripture that came before it, and guarding it in safety: so judge between them by what Allah hath revealed… The goal of you all is to Allah; it is He that will show you the truth of the matters in which ye dispute" (Quran 5:48)

Furthermore, the myths regarding the Quran attacking or copying the Bible are completely dispelled. Instead, the Quran defends the origin of the Bible, and it's Prophets. Helping followers of Judaism and Christianity to be stronger Monotheists and not be swayed by the tensions in the previous scriptures. In addition, the claim of the Noble Quran copying the Bible is disproven;

"It is He Who sent down to thee (step by step), in truth, the Book, confirming what went before it; and He sent down the Law (of Moses) and the Gospel (of Jesus) before this, as a guide to mankind, and He sent down the criterion (of judgment between right and wrong)." (Quran 3:3)

Editor
Mona Ghounem

CONTENTS

Introduction

The Bible was once pure, yet over the centuries, scribal, copyist and linguist errors have caused the divine words to be written, copied, and translated wrong. The Quran cures the human insertions that have caused confusion in the Bible. The Quran mends major manipulations that manifest themselves between the scribes of Moses compared to the scribes of Jesus, causing the fault line between Jews and Christians. Where the Bible makes erroneous single assertions, the Quran counters the contradiction with accurate detailed descriptions. Where the Bible lists multiple conflicting exegeses, the Quran corrects the Bible with a single powerful compendium.

About this book:

This research study is essentially four books in one:

1) A book of **Errancy;** listing over 200 difficulties in the Bible.
2) A book of **Excuses;** listing attempts by the top Biblical apologetics to remedy the errancies.
3) A book of **Rebuttals;** listing refutations to the excuses by Biblicists, so that the reader can make an objective comparison.
4) A book of **Corrections;** listing the miraculous ways the Quran accomplishes what millenniums of Bible scholars could not. In this comprehensive analysis, you will find how the Quran gives clear and concise corrections to Bible errancies.

Overall, this is a book of unity, settling the differences between Jews and Christians:

"And We sent down the Book (Quran) to thee for the express purpose, that thou shouldst make clear to them those things in which they differ, and that it should be a guide and a mercy to those who believe." (Quran 16:64)

The Purpose:

The purpose of this book is multidimensional:

To present harmony to the children of Abraham. Through agreement comes love, and love is the opposite of war. Peaceful tranquility is the effect of the Quran on warring families, neighbors, tribes, countries and religions. The Quran unites over a billion humans from all ethnic and socioeconomic backgrounds, together shoulder to shoulder and foot to foot, in worship to One Creator

To solidify what many Muslims have been stating, that the Quran came to correct the Bible. The Quran is the Divine arbitrator of the Bible, judging between Jews and Christians and being the unifier of the two.

To clarify an often overlooked miracle in the Quran; There are almost a million terms in the entire Bible, hence it's celestially incredible and absolutely impossible to filter through these million words and identify and correct details that were not known to be wrong within the Bible until centuries after the Quran. The Quran, coming from the Lord of the heavens and the earth, accomplishes this divine task for humans to bear witness.

To dispel myths that the Quran copied the Bible. Demonstrating that the Quran is not the copy, it is the correction.

Another myth is that the Quran is from demonic sources. As we will witness, the Quran corrects the Bible on topics of *morality, fairness, and equality* to name a few. God wants us to be moral, just, and equitable, hence the Quran is from God.

How this book was made:

All Praise Due to Allah for the inspiration and time to make this book. Nearly a decade of research has been compiled into this book. Originally, this book was titled "50 Ways...", then as one who initially saw a glitter, I later discovered that the glitter was actually a large treasure trove of corrections from the Quran for the Bible. I was blessed by Allah to find more and more ways, even up to a 101 ways, and then the findings surpassed 200. It is an honor and pleasure to share these findings with you, the reader. Much of the comparative material for this book comes directly from the questions and answers between Bible students and their teachers. Those cycles of (unanswered or poorly answered) questions have caused many to either leave or even rebel against the love of God. The Holy Quran gives the divine answers to those questions and leaves one in complete agreement with mind, heart, and soul.

The Use of Hadeeth

Why Hadeeth were not incorporated in the comparison;

INTRODUCTION

Using Hadeeth (sayings of Prophet Muhammad and his companions) could have possibly given more ways Islamic literature corrected Christian and Judaic literature, but then using Hadeeth would have required a comparison with the Jewish Talmuds (sayings by Rabbis) as well as Encyclicals (sayings by Popes). Therefore, this would delve into second and third person accounts and opinions that would be very controversial and less straight forward than directly comparing our fundamental scriptures; the Bible and the Quran. The authenticity of a few Hadeeths, Talmuds, and Encyclicals are questioned even by their own adherents, some Christians do not believe or adhere to some Encyclicals, and some Jews do not accept some Talmud rulings, therefore it would not be fair to use comparisons that may not be accepted as true by all three religions. Hence, this comparison has been limited to the Quran and Bible.

How to use this book;

We invite the reader both Muslims and non-Muslims to read this book with an open mind, when discussing this book with others, please use it as a tool for unity rather than animosity.

The Rebuttal Chart:

Scholars have tried to make excuses for the discrepant and abnormal passages within the Bible. In the principal of fairness, we are providing the reader with the opportunity to objectively analyze studious excuses by top Biblicists, along with diagnostic Islamic rebuttals to their rationales:

Excuse A: The irrational can be rational at a later time. *When scientists find irrational discoveries, they continue to research the item because a rational explanation may be found at a later time.*
(Reply A)- In principle, this is a valid point, but it has been over 2,000 Years since a Prophet from the Bible has appeared or reappeared. God would not leave 2,000 years of human generations in confusion and unexplainable theological dilemmas. Hence, God has sent the Holy Quran to explain the anomalies in the Bible. God blessed humans with the tools to succeed in this life for this life and the hereafter. What is unexplained in the Bible must be explained. This explanation comes from the Qur'an, the final revelation. When people assume that the unexplainable will never be explained or explained at a later time, then people must look to the Quran for immediate clarification and a fulfillment of the void.

Excuse B: Humans cannot fully understand the Revelation of God, unless the spirit of God is with us.

Because humans are imperfect, we cannot perfectly interpret what God says.

(Reply B)- This is a circular argument based on (1 Corinthians 2:14) "the natural man receiveth not the things of the Spirit of God for they are foolishness to him; neither can he know them for they are spiritually discerned." This has led us to the conclusion that one would need to be in a certain spiritually altered state of mind, a self-hypnosis that the Bible is true.

It is unacceptable that one has to be in a mental stupor to accept the Bible. When the mind is clear of internal or external intoxicants, only then can we judge clearly between the Truth and distortion. (1 Corinthians 14:33) "For God is not the author of confusion"

Excuse C: You must understand the context of the verse.

(Reply C)- This is a false claim because there are an abundant amount of chapters in the Bible that contain no context, for example; Proverbs. The verses are a number of independent statements that skip through different subjects. Other examples include the discrepancies between Samuel, Kings, and Chronicles, which contain verses about people, and numbers, which invalidate the out of context argument.

Excuse D: A vital word is difficult to interpret because it's rarely used in the Bible

(Reply D)- Everything in Scripture is important for human beings. Our guidance from God comes from scripture. If scripture is not clear in an obscure passage, then we can not just skip past that passage or try to conclude it's meaning to another plain passage. Furthermore, the Quran was given to us to clear the obscurity that is found within the Bible.

Excuse E; That's what it says but that's not what it means

(Reply E)- If the Bible writers meant something else, then why didn't they record it as it was meant? Were their pens prevented from writing what the scribes meant? Those who use this excuse claim they know Greek and Hebrew better than the ancient Greek and Hebrew writers in Biblical times. The Bible translators utilize a vast amount of vocabulary dictionaries and ancient texts to pick the exact interpretation. In turn, the process itself of choosing Biblical words, invalidate their excuse.

Excuse F: Copyist Error

(Reply F)- This is another unacceptable excuse because it is admitting the Bible we have today has human errors, hence not a divine book.

For example, an item is either made in China or made in the USA, it can not be made in both places, unless it's transported between the two, at that point, it's no longer 100% Chinese or all American, it's diluted and hence no longer 100% authentic.

Excuse G; Later Scripture replaces Previous Scripture.

(Reply G)- If this is true, then over a billion Muslims state that the Quran, which came after the Bible, supersedes past revelations (Torah and Gospel). The fact is, God promised to Abraham that the covenant of Laws is forever and everlasting, as well as Jesus himself declaring he did not come to change the laws; "Do not think that I came to destroy the Law or the Prophets. I did not come to destroy but to fulfill. For verily I say unto you, Till heaven and earth pass, one jot or one title shall in no wise pass from the law, till all be fulfilled. " (Matthew 5:17-18).

Excuse H; Existing Biblical words are being taken literally instead of symbolically or metaphorically.

(Reply H)- Apologetics try to fall back on this excuse when common sense fails. An entire sentence is claimed to be literal except for the divergent word in the sentence, at which that one errant word is categorized as "metaphorical". We cannot selectively choose which words in a sentence or scenario are figurative while the surrounding words in the sentence and chapter are literal.

Excuse I; Translation error

(Reply I)- Apologetics admit that some of the errors in the Bible are attributed to translation errors from Hebrew to Greek to German to English. Of course, any linguist would also admit that no word could be perfectly translated from one language to another, especially from one language funneled down through four languages.

This may be acceptable in earthly texts, but this excuse is unacceptable in Divine Scripture, especially in the light of the Quran. This excuse is corrected by the Quran because the Quran is only accepted as authentic in its original language (Arabic). Yet, Bible apologetics want us to still believe that the Bible is Divine and inerrant in every language of the world when that is linguistically impossible, and at the same time, Biblicists confess that there are translation errors in the Bible.

(I.) God

The Omniscient and Omnipotent, Creator of Everything including our thoughts!

1. <u>Needing Composure?</u>

Errancy; Within the following passage, the Bible clearly errs in stating that God rests.

"By the seventh day God had finished the work he had been doing; so on the seventh day he rested from all his work. And God blessed the seventh day and made it holy, because on it he rested from all the work of creating that he had done" (Genesis 2:2).

Bible narrators took the idea that God rested further still when they wrote as follows:

"In six days the Lord made heaven and earth, and on the seventh day he rested, and was refreshed" (Exodus 31: 17)

Excuse; Mistranslation.

Rebuttal: (See Reply letter [I] in Rebuttal Chart)

Correction: According to the Quran, God does not display any human attributes of weakness or fatigue, and hence, does not need rest. This false claim of God needing rest is corrected in God's own words when God declared:

"And verily we created the heavens and the earth and all that is between them in six periods, and naught of weariness touched us" (Quran 50:38).

According to the Holy Quran, the Final Testament, God does not get tired "Neither slumber nor sleep overtakes Him" (Quran 2:255).

2. <u>Needing Food?</u>

Errancy; God eats solid food with Abraham. (Genesis 18:1-8)

Excuse; Abraham's visitors were just men or angels, God was not with them.

Rebuttal: According to the *Matthew Henry Complete Commentary* on (Genesis 18:1-18), God was one of the visitors who ate with Abraham.

Correction: God is Self Sufficient and beyond needing or wanting any of the things that sustain a human to live, such as food. Here we see that God corrects what is written in Genesis by declaring within the Quran:

"Say: 'Shall I take for my protector any other than Allah, the Maker of the heavens and the earth? And He it is that feedeth but is not fed." (Quran 6:14)

3. Needing Sleep?

Errancy; "Then the Lord awaked as one out of sleep and like a mighty man that shouts by reason of wine. (Psalm 78:65)

"Awake, why do you sleep, O Lord?" (Psalms 44:23)

Excuse; None available.

Correction: Where would we be if God needed to sleep? God in the Quran is depicted in a true light when He, The Almighty is describing Himself by stating: "Neither slumber nor sleep overtakes Him" (Quran 2:255)

4. In Darkness or Light?

Errancy; Within the Bible, there is a contradiction that states God dwells in thick darkness (1 Kings 8:12) and then in another verse, we read: God dwells in unapproachable light. (1 Timothy 6:16)

Excuse; Figures of speech and need not be taken literally

Rebuttal: (See Reply letter [H] in Rebuttal Chart) God is speaking to humans, not nocturnal creatures who perceive light and darkness differently than humans. In light of the scripture being sent down to humans, we must ascertain the verses are to be interpreted literally, as humans understand them. For example, if the Bible was sent to earth for the bats, and other nocturnal creatures, then we would interpret light to mean darkness, since this is not the case, light to us humans should and does logically means light.

Correction: In the following verses, we see how being in the dark is not a place where we should even be, let alone imagine our Lord, Most High to be:

"These are they who purchase error at the price of guidance, so their commerce doth not prosper, neither are they guided. Their likeness is as the likeness of one who kindleth fire, and when it sheddeth its light around him Allah taketh away their light and leaveth them in darkness, where they cannot see." (Quran 2:16-17)

"Allah is the Protector of those who have faith: from the depths of darkness He will lead them forth into light. Of those who reject faith the patrons are the evil ones: from light, they will lead them forth into the depths of darkness. They will be companions of the fire, to dwell therein (For ever)." (Quran 2:257)

"O people of the Scripture! Now hath Our messenger come unto you, expounding unto you much of that which ye used to hide in the Scripture, and forgiving much. Now hath come unto you light from Allah and a plain Scripture Whereby Allah guideth him who seeketh His good pleasure unto paths of peace. He bringeth them out of darkness unto light by His decree, and guideth them unto a straight path." (Quran 5: 15-16)

Thus, we see the path to Allah is the path to light, and the path away from Allah is the path to darkness. This contrast clarifies that God dwells in light in the Quran, unlike in the Bible.

5. Making Mistakes?

Errancy; The Bible shows an ongoing pattern of humanizing God, stating;

"And the Lord was sorry that he made man on the earth, and it grieved him to his heart. [he said]: For I am sorry that I have made them." (Genesis 6:6-7)

Excuse; All humans are sinners; therefore, God is not happy with his creation.

Rebuttal: Adding injury to insult, Biblical apologetics not only insult God by claiming God was ignorant towards the future state of humans, but they also claim all humans are sinners, even though the Bible states that some humans were perfect. Our Omniscient God knows the future and does not regret any actions taken or feel remorse for His magnificent creations. No, God does not make mistakes. The Holy Quran corrects the notion that was conceived from the Bible; implying that we as humans were a mistake and not meant to be created. The truth has come by God who clearly stated to us in the Holy Quran that we are meant to be alive. All praise be to God.

Correction: The Quran restores the fulfillment of destiny in regards to God's creations by stating:

"My Lord Never Errs, Nor Forgets" (Quran 20:52)

In conclusion, we are created without regret. We are here today because God is compassionate towards us and does not regret creating us.

6. God can be seen?

Errancy; There is a discrepancy in the Bible about whether God has been seen or not. The Christians, based on the assumption that Jesus is God, claim we have seen God, in flesh form.

Furthermore, the Bible lists some Prophets who have seen God before Jesus came to earth;

"And I will take away my hand, and thou shalt see my back parts." (Exodus 33:23)

"And the Lord spoke to Moses face to face, as a man speaketh to his friend." (Exodus 33:11)

"For I have seen God face to face, and my life is preserved." (Genesis 32:30)

Vs

No one has ever seen God (Exodus 33:17, 20, John 1:18, 1 Timothy 6:15-16)

Excuse; People were seeing visions, or dreams, or the Angel of the Lord (Numbers 22:22-26; Judges 13:1-21) and not really God Himself.

Rebuttal: Those cited passages do not say 'vision, dream, or Angel' of the Lord, they say that people saw God (Exodus 24:9-11), that God was seen, and that He appeared as God (Exodus 6:2-3).

Correction: Some Christians claim they need to see Jesus (in graven images such as crosses, paintings, and statues), to believe and or to remember God exists. In response to this, all of nature is proof that God exists.

Furthermore, how can we withstand the magnificent sight of our God who created the Sun and all the other stars in the Universe?

The Lord of the heavens and the earth is too brilliant for our eyes to view Him in this life. Even Prophets have not been able to see Him as God says to Moses in this verse:

"When Moses came at Our appointed time and his Lord spoke to him, he said: My Lord! show me (Thyself), so that I may look upon Thee. He said: You cannot (bear to) see Me but look at the mountain, if it remains firm in its place, then will you see Me; but when his Lord manifested His glory to the mountain He made it crumble and Moses fell down in a swoon; then when he recovered, he said: Glory be to Thee, I turn to Thee, and I am the first of the believers." (Quran 7:143)

God is Exalted from those who make pictures and idols stating that it is God, when they are falsely describing He who we cannot see:

"Glorified be the Lord of the heavens and the earth, the Lord of the Throne! Exalted is He from all that they ascribe (to Him)." (Quran 43:82)

"Verily! Those who fear their Lord unseen, theirs will be forgiveness and a great reward" (Quran 67:12)

We now understand that our human sensors could not glimpse the Originator of the Universe.

7. God remembers all?

Errancy; The Bible demonstrates God as forgetful;

"Why do you forget us forever, why do you so long forsake us?" (Lamentations 5:20)

"How long will You Forget me, O Lord" (Psalms 13:1)

Excuse; None available.

Correction: The Quran explains to us that God remembers all:

"(The angels say :) "We descend not but by command of thy Lord: to Him belongeth what is before us and what is behind us, and what is between: and thy Lord never doth forget " (Quran 19:64)

"My Lord Never Errs, Nor Forgets" (Quran 20:52)

8. <u>God Weak in Wrestling?</u>

Errancy; In the Bible, God is not described to be the Most Powerful. Instead, God is described to be weak and powerless.

In (Genesis 32:24-30), God is characterized as wrestling with Jacob all night long, losing the match;

"And Jacob was left alone; and there wrestled a man with him until the breaking of the day. And when he saw that he prevailed not against him, he touched the hollow of his thigh; and the hollow of Jacob's thigh was out of joint, as he wrestled with him."

"And he said, Let me go, for the day breaketh. And he said, I will not let thee go, except thou bless me. And he said unto him, What is thy name? And he said, Jacob And he said, Thy name shall be called no more Jacob, but Israel: for as a prince hast thou power with God and with men, and hast prevailed."

"And Jacob asked him, and said, Tell me, I pray thee, thy name. And he said, Wherefore is it that thou dost ask after my name? And he blessed him there. And Jacob called the name of the place Peniel: for I have seen God face to face, and my life is preserved." (Genesis 32:24-30)

Excuse; The *Jamieson, Fausset, Brown Bible Commentary* makes the excuse that Jacob saw an opportunity to squeeze a blessing out of God and took advantage of God's vulnerability;

"It is evident that Jacob was aware of the character of Him with whom he wrestled; and, believing that His power, though by far superior to human, was yet limited by His promise to do him good, he determined not to lose the golden opportunity of securing a blessing. And nothing gives God greater pleasure than to see the hearts of His people firmly adhering to Him." (*JFB commentary on Genesis 32:26*)

Rebuttal: This confirms the humanization of God in the Bible.

Correction: God is Omnipotent and cannot be beaten by a human as God's true nature is described in the Quran:

"It is He Who begins (the process of) creation; then repeats it; and for Him it is most easy. To Him belongs the loftiest similitude (we can think of) in the heavens and the earth: for He is Exalted in Might, Full of Wisdom." (Quran 30:27)

"Seest thou not that Allah created the heavens and the earth in Truth? If He so will, He can remove you and put (in your place) a new Creation?" (Quran 14:19)

Within those verses of the Quran, we find the corrected attributes of God. If God had wanted to, He could have eliminated Jacob, and He could have wiped out all the people. Thus, God in the Quran does not lose against humans.

9. Moving Iron?

Errancy; God cannot move iron; "And the Lord was with Judah; and he drove out the inhabitants of the mountain; but could not drive out the inhabitants of the valley, because they had chariots of iron." (Judges 1:19)

Excuse; God did not want to move the iron because Judah's army was disobedient.

Rebuttal: Biblical apologetics contradict themselves by saying that the promise to Judah was conditional; hence, God purposefully did not move the iron (even though no hint of this scenario is mentioned in the passage). While in other excuses, the promise to Judah is unconditional; (Judges 1:19) clearly states that God did indeed 'help Judah's army and drove out the inhabitants of the mountain', hence there was no animosity between God and the army of Judah, thus invalidating this excuse.

Correction: Nothing of God's creation is too powerful for God to destroy:

"And the day on which We will cause the mountains to pass away and you will see the earth a leveled plain and We will gather them and leave not any one of them behind." (Quran 18:47)

"They will ask thee of the mountains (on that day). Say: My Lord will break them into scattered dust." (Quran 20:105)

10. God's Reputation?

Errancy; The Bible displays God as a hesitating human concerned about what other humans may think regarding the actions taken to enforce the Law. Although laws were broken, in the Bible, it shows God resists evoking Justice based on God's reputation being tarnished;

"But they rebelled against me and would not listen to me; they did not get rid of the vile images they had set their eyes on, nor did they forsake the idols of Egypt. So I said I would pour out my wrath on them and spend my anger against them in Egypt. But for the sake of my name I did what would keep it from being profaned in the eyes of the nations they lived among and in whose sight I had revealed myself to the Israelites by bringing them out of Egypt. Therefore I led them out of Egypt and brought them into the desert." (Ezekiel 20:8-10)

Excuse; None available.

Correction: As the Bible displays a worrisome God being profaned by Israelites, the Quran brings a clearer light in showing a confident and consistently equitable God.

"Yet there are men who take (for worship) others besides Allah, as equal (with Allah): They love them as they should love Allah. But those of Faith are overflowing in their love for Allah. If only the unrighteous could see, behold, they would see the penalty: that to Allah belongs all power, and Allah will strongly enforce the penalty." (Quran 2:165)

11. Looking for Adam

Errancy; God does not see everything and is not omnipresent (Genesis 3:8-10)

Excuse; God became a visible manifestation, hence was no longer everywhere.

Rebuttal: This is something Christians never grasped; God means God. The All Knowing, The All Hearing and The All Seeing can and does know everything, everywhere at the same time. Sounds impossible? That is why we call Him God.

Correction: God is always aware of what is hidden and seen within the heavens and earth. God sees our lives before we do and God see our inner most thoughts before we think them, so how can it be that God cannot see everything.

"Seest thou not that Allah doth know (all) that is in the heavens and on earth? There is not a secret consultation between three, but He makes the fourth among them, - Nor between five but He makes the sixth, - nor between fewer nor more, but He is in their midst, wheresoever they be: In the end will He tell them the truth of their conduct, on the Day of Judgment. For Allah has full knowledge of all things." (Quran 58:7)

12. The Lord of Earth?

Errancy; God is the Lord of earth (Psalms 24:1, 1 Corinthians 10:26) *Vs* The earth is the devil's kingdom (John 12:31, 2 Corinthians 4:4)

Excuse; None available.

Correction: God is the Ruler of the Earth and the Heavens and God does not allow the devil to roam, tempting man, without God's decree.

"Unto Allah belongeth the Sovereignty of the heavens and the earth. Allah is Able to do all things. Lo! In the creation of the heavens and the earth and (in) the difference of night and day are tokens (of His sovereignty) for men of understanding, (Quran 3:189-190)

13. God Near?

Errancy; God is always near (Psalms 46:1, 145:14, 18-19, James 4:8) *Vs* God is not always near (1 Samuel 28:6, Psalms 10:1, 22:1-2, Matthew 27:46)

Excuse; None available.

Correction: "God is closer to us than our own veins: We verily created a man and We know what his soul whispereth to him, and We are nearer to him than his jugular vein." (Quran 50:16)

14. Standing to Judge?

Errancy; God sits to Judge people (Joel 3:12) *Vs* God stands to Judge people (Isaiah 3:13)

Excuse; God sits to listen to each case and then stands to make the Judgment.

Rebuttal: The Bible does not say, "After hearing the cases, God stands from the Throne to Judge."

Furthermore, it is far-fetched to claim that God sits and stands billions of times for billions of humans; even human Judges do not sit and stand during court cases. (Isaiah 3:13) suggests it is a consistent standing while Biblical apologetics would like us to think God performs bionic aerobics on Judgment Day. Lastly, God is above all humans, so there is no need to stand.

Correction: "Your Guardian-Lord is Allah, Who created the heavens and the earth in six periods, and is firmly established on the throne (of authority)" (Quran 7:54)

"And thou wilt see the angels surrounding the Throne (Divine) on all sides, singing Glory and Praise to their Lord. The Decision between them (at Judgment) will be in (perfect) justice, and the cry (on all sides) will be, "Praise be to Allah, the Lord of the Worlds!" (Quran 39:75)

"His Throne doth extend over the heavens and the earth, and He feeleth no fatigue in guarding and preserving them for He is the Most High, the Supreme (in glory)." (Quran 2:255)

Thus, the Throne of God is above all, showing no reason to stand for judgments.

15. Collective Punishment

Errancy; God does not punish the children for the sins of the parents (Ezekiel 18:20) *Vs* "the iniquity of the fathers on the children to the third and fourth generations". (Exodus 20:5)

Excuse; Guilt is not passed on but consequences are.

Rebuttal: First, (Ezekiel 18:20) does not differentiate between guilt or consequence, only inequity and righteousness. Second, guilt in many cases is as bad as or worse than the consequences, for example; Edgar Allen Poe's story "The Tell Tale Heart." Third, many other verses from the Bible do not differentiate with which aspect of sin is not passed; (Jeremiah 31:30), (Psalms 49:7), (Deuteronomy 24:16)

Correction: God only punishes those who are transgressors and disbelievers. In contrast to the Bible, God does not collectively punish in the Quran.

"Who receiveth guidance, receiveth it for his own benefit: who goeth astray doth so to his own loss: No bearer of burdens can bear the burden of another: nor would We visit with Our Wrath until We had sent an messenger (to give warning)." (Quran 17:15)

16. Destroying the World Again?

Errancy; "…I will not again curse the ground any more for man's sake; for the imagination of man's heart is evil from his youth; neither will I again smite any more every thing living, as I have done." (Genesis 8:21) *Vs* "the heavens will pass away with a great noise, and the elements will melt with fervent heat; both the earth and the works that are in it will be burned up" (2 Peter 3:10).

Excuse; Biblical apologetics grasp at straws by claiming what God meant was that the same flood method would not be used again; "as I have done."

Rebuttal: What the passage actually reads is "neither will I again smite any more every thing living, as I have done" not as I have done with water or I will smite everything living in a different way next time. In a logical interpretation without making false insertions, this passage says, "I killed all before and I won't do it again". "as I have done" is a confession, not an omission of genocide tactics for the presumed next time.

Correction: First, there has never yet been destruction to all people according to the Quran. God does not destroy innocent people and will save those whom He will.

The option is open for God to destroy the sinners;

"Seest thou not that Allah created the heavens and the earth in Truth? If He so will, He can remove you and put (in your place) a new Creation?" (Quran 14:19)

Therefore, God in the Quran does not make any contradictory promises as in the Bible. The Quran displays an open option for our Just God to do as He wills.

17. Vanity

Errancy; "Let us make man in our own image" (Genesis 1:26)

Excuse; None available

Correction: Certainly, the creations cannot be like the Creator and the Creator is not like His creations. Exalted is God, far above the creations of the heaven and earth as the Quran states: "There is none like Him!" (Quran 112:4)

18. Merciful?

Errancy; God in the Bible orders his followers in a battle to kill every living thing including, women, children, and animals, demonstrating a disproportionate, merciless, collective punishment;

"Thus says the Lord of hosts, 'I will punish what Am'alek did to Israel in opposing them on the way, when they came up out of Egypt. Go and attack the Amalekites and completely destroy everything they have. Don't leave a thing; kill all the men, women, children, and babies; the cattle, sheep, camels, and donkeys." (1 Samuel 15:2–3)

Excuse; None available.

Correction: God orders Muslims in the Quran to have patience against those who attack you, and if the attacks persist, we are only to retaliate with the same amount we were attacked with and to never go beyond the amount of attack we received:

"And if you take your turn, then retaliate with the like of that with which you were afflicted; But if ye endure patiently, verily it is better for the patient." (Quran 16:126)

19. Indecent Proposal

Errancy; God commands Isaiah to go naked for 3 years (Isaiah 20:1-3, Amos 2:16)

Excuse; None available.

Correction: God does not command anything shameful:

"When they do aught that is shameful, they say: "We found our fathers doing so"; and "Allah commanded us thus": Say: "Nay, Allah never commands what is shameful: do ye say of Allah what ye know not?" (Quran 7:28)

(II.)   Prophets

Best of Humans filled with the message and power from God.
Our Messengers and Examples of Righteousness

20. <u>Moses Killed Because of Sin ?</u>

Errancy; All three Monotheistic faiths revere Moses as a Righteous
Prophet. Followers of Judaism even revere Moses to be the greatest
Prophet of Israel and to Christians, Moses is compared to Jesus.
Likewise, Muslims profess that Muhammad (peace be upon him) is the
foretold Prophet (Deuteronomy 18:18) "similar to Moses".

Yet, the Bible reports that Moses was stricken with a humiliating death
by God. (Deuteronomy 32:51) says Moses "broke faith" with God;

"The Lord spoke to Moses that very same day saying, "Go up to this
mountain of the Abarim, Mount Nebo, which is in the land of Moab
opposite Jericho, and look at the land of Canaan, which I am giving to
the sons of Israel for a possession."

"Then die on the mountain where you ascend, and be gathered to your
people, as Aaron your brother died on Mount Hor and was gathered to
his people, because you broke faith with Me in the midst of the sons of
Israel at the waters of Meribah-kadesh, in the wilderness of Zin,"

"because you did not treat Me as holy in the midst of the sons of Israel.
For you shall see the land at a distance, but you shall not go there, into
the land which I am giving the sons of Israel." (Deuteronomy 32:48-52)

The Bible delineates a torturous death to a Prophet who devoted his life
to God. Prophet Moses could have inherited the throne of Pharaoh;
instead, Moses turned away the riches and pleasures of Pharaoh for God.
Moses put his life in danger by single handedly fighting the army of
Pharaoh; at all times having faith, God would protect him. Moses also
spent decades trying to lead the rebellious Israelites through the
scorching desert.

Do the Bible writers really think that God would send his wrath upon
Moses for his choice of going from a wealthy heir of Pharaoh to a
humble prophet, by killing him? What is also cruel about the death of
Moses is that he was reminded of his two loves before the murder, Moses
was reminded of the death of his brother Aaron, and of the land, Moses is
never to enter, Israel.

Excuse; Bible commentators try to justify the death of Moses with the following points; (1) Striking the rock rather than speaking to it. (2) Speaking to the people instead of speaking to the rock. (3) Speaking to the people harshly and calling them "rebels" (4) Taking credit for the act rather than giving the credit to God, "shall we bring forth water for you out of this rock" (Numbers 20:10).

Rebuttal: The passage in the Bible commanding Moses to speak to the rock contradicts earlier verses in the Bible;

"Behold, I will stand before thee there upon the rock in Horeb; and thou shalt smite the rock, and there shall come water out of it that the people may drink. And Moses did so in the sight of the elders of Israel." (Exodus 17:6)

Hence, Moses has a history and pattern of striking the rock and therefore he was killed according to the Bible for obeying what God told him to do.

Correction: The Holy Quran keeps the integrity of Moses and does not affirm his murder. The Quran honors Moses until the end, and does not give him the horrible murder as the Bible does;

"We divided them into twelve tribes or nations. We directed Moses by inspiration, when his (thirsty) people asked him for water: "Strike the rock with thy staff": out of it there gushed forth twelve springs: Each group knew its own place for water. We gave them the shade of clouds, and sent down to them manna and quails, (saying): "Eat of the good things We have provided for you": (but they rebelled); to Us they did no harm, but they harmed their own souls." (Quran 7:160)

"And (remember) when Moses asked for water for his people, We said: "Strike the stone with your stick." Then gushed forth there from twelve springs. Each (group of) people knew its own place for water. "Eat and drink of that which Allah has provided and do not act corruptly, making mischief on the earth." (Quran 2:60)

Here the Quran states that Moses was indeed loyal and did in fact follow directions; the true and logical directions for extracting water from the rock was to hit the rock, not "speak" to the rock to gush forth the water.

In conclusion, Moses has consistently struck the rock to get water in the past. Moses has consistently obeyed God in the past. The cruel, anguishing murder for not speaking to a rock is inconsistent with God's laws of mercy, logic, and protection of his Prophets.

The Quran resolves the inconsistency in the Bible by revealing Moses was never told to 'speak to the rock'. Instead, Moses was only told to strike the rock as ordered in the past. Moses also obeys God by getting the life saving water in the desert for the Israelites. Therefore, God rewards Moses and his honor is saved in the Quran.

21. Did Aaron worship Idols?

Errancy; In the Biblical version, almost all prophets seem to commit major sins in faith and moral standing. Within the Bible, some of the shameful deeds attributed to prophets include; Aaron's idol worship;

"Aaron said to people of Israel, 'take off the rings of Gold which are in the ears of your wives, your sons and your daughters.' So they took off the rings of gold, and brought them to Aaron. And he received the golf at their hand and fashioned it with a graving tool and made a molten calf and they said, "These are your Gods, O Israel, who brought you up out of the land of Egypt." (Exodus. 32:2)

Excuse; None available.

Correction: The Biblical concept of prophet hood is also radically different from the one presented in the Quran. The Quran depicts prophets as the best model of piety and moral uprightness. The Quran refutes this claim against Aaron;

"(Allah) said: 'We have tested thy people in thy absence: the Samiri has led them astray.' So Moses returned to his people in a state of indignation and sorrow. He said: "O my people! did not your Lord make a handsome promise to you? Did then the promise seem to you long (in coming)? Or did ye desire that Wrath should descend from your Lord on you, and so ye broke your promise to me?"

"They said: 'We broke not the promise to thee, as far as lay in our power: but we were made to carry the weight of the ornaments of the (whole) people, and we threw them (into the fire), and that was what the Samiri suggested.

"Then he brought out (of the fire) before the (people) the image of a calf: It seemed to low: so they said: This is your god, and the god of Moses, but (Moses) has forgotten! Could they not see that it could not return them a word (for answer), and that it had no power either to harm them or to do them good?"

"Aaron had already, before this said to them: "O my people! ye are being tested in this: for verily your Lord is (Allah) Most Gracious; so follow me and obey my command. They had said: "We will not abandon this cult, but we will devote ourselves to it until Moses returns to us. (Moses) said: "O Aaron! what kept thee back, when thou sawest them going wrong, from following me? Didst thou then disobey my order?"

"(Aaron) replied: "O son of my mother! Seize (me) not by my beard nor by (the hair of) my head! Truly I feared lest thou shouldst say, 'Thou has caused a division among the children of Israel, and thou didst not respect my word!'" (Quran 20:85-94)

The Quran clears Aaron of participation in the making and worshipping of the golden calf as the Bible portrays. The Quran illuminates the fact that Aaron was simply not as strong as Moses, being the younger and weaker brother of Moses; Aaron could not control the Israelites as Moses could, despite pleas by Aaron for the Israelites to stop.

"Not a messenger did We send before thee without this inspiration sent by Us to him: that there is no god but I; therefore worship and serve Me. And they say: "(Allah) Most Gracious has begotten offspring." Glory to Him! They are (but) servants raised to honor. They speak not before He speaks, and they act (in all things) by His Command." (Quran 21:25-27)

22. Prophet David

Errancy; According to the Bible, David committed voyeurism and adultery with the wife of Uriah, and had her husband killed (2 Samuel 11:2-15)

"David arose from his couch and was walking upon the roof that he saw from the roof a woman bathing; and the woman was very beautiful, and David sent and inquired about the woman. And one said, "Is not that Bathshe'ba, the daughter of Eli'am, the wife of Uri'ah the Hittite?"

So David sent messengers and took her, and she came to him and he lay with her. Then she returned to her house; and she sent and told David, I am with child. David called her husband, and invited him, and ate in his presence and drank, so that he made him drunk. In the morning David wrote to Jo'ab, "Set Uri'ah in the forefront of the hardest fighting, and then draw back from him, that he may be struck down and die."

Excuse; None available.

Correction: The inspired Prophet David, who was entrusted with Holy Scripture, was sent on earth to be a guide to human beings and not to display vain desires as the Bible depicts Prophet David as doing:

"Lo! We inspire thee as We inspired Noah and the prophets after him, as We inspired Abraham and Ishmael and Isaac and Jacob and the tribes, and Jesus and Job and Jonah and Aaron and Solomon, and as we imparted unto David the Psalms;" (Quran 4:163)

"And We bestowed upon him Isaac and Jacob; each of them We guided; and Noah did We guide aforetime; and of his seed (We guided) David and Solomon and Job and Joseph and Moses and Aaron. Thus do We reward the good? And Zachariah and John and Jesus and Elias. Each one (of them) was of the righteous." (Quran 6:84-85)

23. Curse of Jesus?

Errancy; Anyone who calls another a fool is liable to Hell. (Matthew 5:22)

Vs

Jesus says that anyone who hears his words and does not do them is a fool. (Matthew 7:26)

In (Matthew 23:17-19), Jesus twice calls the Pharisees blind fools.

In (Matthew 25:2-3, 8), Jesus compares the maidens who took no oil to fools.

Excuse; That is what it says but that is not what it means

Rebuttal: (See Reply letter [E] in Rebuttal Chart) The word "fool" has no dual meaning. Whether the phrase is said angrily or softly, (which Jesus said in both tones), the word still has the same meaning.

Correction: God gave wisdom, among other high attributes to Jesus to guide folk to the straight path. Whether the people believed in the truth readily or were still unbelievers, Jesus was free from being one who mocked others.

The Quran clarifies that Jesus was upright, honorable, and spoke the Good News from Allah, not profanity:

"I have come unto you with wisdom, and to make plain some of that concerning which ye differ. So keep your duty to Allah, and obey me." (Quran 43:63)

"Then We caused Our messengers to follow in their footsteps; and We caused Jesus, son of Mary, to follow, and gave him the Gospel, and placed compassion and mercy in the hearts of those who followed him. But monasticism they invented. We ordained it not for them. Only seeking Allah's pleasure, and they observed it not with right observance. So We give those of them who believe their reward, but many of them are evil livers." (Quran 57:27)

"O ye who believe! Be Allah's helpers, even as Jesus son of Mary said unto the disciples: Who are my helpers for Allah? They said: We are Allah's helpers. And a party of the Children of Israel believed, while a party disbelieved. Then We strengthened those who believed against their foe, and they became the uppermost." (Quran 61:14)

24. Cain's Crime?

Errancy; According to the Bible, Adam's son; Cain committed a murder against his brother Abel and was not punished for that crime (Genesis 4:12-16)

Excuse; God had not yet established capital punishment

Rebuttal: The problem with this excuse is that the Bible does not specify "Thou shall not kill" until (Exodus 20:13) hence, readers are bewildered as to why Cain is freed.

Correction: The Quran clarifies why and when the Law of "Thou Shall not Kill" was given while the Bible leaves readers presuming the law is already known, hence the assumption that Cain gets away with murder:

"And relate to them the story of the two sons of Adam with truth when they both offered an offering, but it was accepted from one of them and was not accepted from the other. He said: I will most certainly slay you. (The other) said: Allah only accepts from those who guard (against evil)." (Quran 5:27)

"If you will stretch forth your hand towards me to slay me, I am not one to stretch forth my hand towards you to slay you surely I fear Allah, the Lord of the worlds:" (Quran 5:28)

"Surely I wish that you should bear the sin committed against me and your own sin, and so you would be of the inmates of the fire, and this is the recompense of the unjust." (Quran 5:29)

"But (the other's) mind imposed on him the killing of his brother, so he slew him and became one of the losers." (Quran 5:30)

"Then Allah sent a crow digging up the earth so that he might show him how he should cover the dead body of his brother. He said: Woe me! do I lack the strength that I should be like this crow and cover the dead body of my brother? So he became of those who regret."

"For this reason did We prescribe to the children of Israel that whoever slays a soul, unless it be for manslaughter or for mischief in the land, it is as though he slew all men; and whoever keeps it alive, it is as though he kept alive all men; and certainly Our messengers came to them with clear arguments, but even after that many of them certainly act extravagantly in the land." (Quran 5:27-32)

25. Where was Moses Called?

Errancy; Moses called by God in Egypt (Exodus 3:10) *Vs* Moses called by God in Midian (Exodus 4:19)

Excuse; (Exodus 6) was a reconfirmation of the call by God to Moses because Moses was reluctant the first time.

Rebuttal: Moses was a loyal and faithful Prophet who obeyed God from the moment he was commissioned by God. Furthermore, (Exodus 6) does not hint at all of being a reconfirmation or a reminder.

Correction: The Quran corrects the scenario of the Biblically depicted forgetful and regretful Prophet by describing that Moses had already left Egypt, when he was called by God to go back to the land of Pharaoh:

Moses was not in Egypt when God called on him because Moses was charged with a crime in Egypt and stayed out of Egypt to avoid persecution; (Quran 26:14)

Then after God blessed Moses, Moses returned to the land of Pharaoh:

"So I fled from you (all) when I feared you; but my Lord has (since) invested me with judgment (and wisdom) and appointed me as one of the messengers." (Quran 26:21)

26. Prophet or Spirit?

Errancy; There is confusion in the Bible regarding Jesus' criterion;

"I have yet many things to say unto you, but ye cannot bear them now. Howbeit when he, the Spirit of truth, is come, he will guide you into all truth: for he shall not speak of himself; but whatsoever he shall hear, that shall he speak: and he will show you things to come." (John 16:12-13)

While Jesus is clearly speaking of a person, Christians claim Jesus is foretelling the Holy Spirit.

Many see (John 16:12-13) as one of the many predictions of Prophet Muhammad (peace be upon him) and the -prediction- of the Holy Quran as this research makes evident.

Excuse; That is what it says but that is not what it means. This is a prediction about the Holy Spirit, not Muhammad (peace be upon him).

Rebuttal: (See Reply letter [E] in Rebuttal Chart). First, Trinitarians claim that the Holy Spirit, God, and Jesus are all one entity while Jesus was obviously speaking of someone other than himself in (John 16:12-13). Jesus spoke about himself in (v12) "I have" then switches from personal pronouns "I" to "he", rather then maintaining a constant personal pronoun of "I". Jesus does not say; "I will come later to finish speaking".

Secondly, we know that the Holy Spirit and Jesus are not one in the same because of (Matthew 12:31);

"Wherefore I say unto you, all manner of sin and blasphemy shall be forgiven unto men: but the blasphemy against the Holy Ghost shall not be forgiven unto men."

Yet after the thief next to Jesus on the cross -mocked and reviled- Jesus (Mark 15:32), Jesus forgave one and said you will go to Heaven (Luke 23:43).

Third, Jesus admits that he has nothing else to say; Jesus states that everything his Creator wanted him to say was already said;

"for all things that I have heard of my Father I have made known unto you." (John 15:15)

Which confirms an individual other than Jesus will say more. For example; it would be a symptom of schizophrenia for someone to say; "I said everything I was told, and I will come to say more from me and I will glorify myself and I will say nothing of my own will other than what I was told by myself".

One has a free choice of following the Trinitarians' perplexity or believing that (John 16:12-13) was the logical prediction of Prophet Muhammad (peace be upon him) because our loving God would not leave us for over 2,000 years with no other guidance.

Correction: God in the Quran confirms that (John 16:12-13) was indeed predicting Muhammad; (peace be upon him)

"…whom they will find described in the Torah and the Gospel (which are) with them. He will enjoin on them that which is right and forbid them that which is wrong. He will make lawful for them all good things and prohibit for them only the foul…" (Quran 7:157)

Indeed, we find this is the exact description of Prophet Muhammad, foretold in the Bible, and correcting the wrong, and removing previous dietary curses while maintaining prohibitions on the foul such as swine.

27. The One Who Recites

Errancy; There is a two thousand year old void in the Bible regarding an expected prophet. The prophecy is of an unlearned man, given divine scripture;

"And the book is delivered to him that is not learned, saying, Read this, I pray thee: and he saith, I am not learned." (Isaiah 29:12)

Many see (Isaiah 29:12) as one of the many predictions of Prophet Muhammad (peace be upon him) and the (prediction of the) Holy Quran as this research makes evident.

Excuse; You must understand the context of the verse.

Rebuttal: (See Reply letter [C] in Rebuttal Chart). The context here is speaking of various predictions with no coherent single subject matter.

Correction: The Holy Quran fills the voids within the Bible by verifying that Prophet Muhammad (peace be upon him) was indeed the foretold one who will recite the Holy Book:

"Those who follow the messenger, the Prophet who can neither read nor write, whom they will find described in the Torah and the Gospel (which are) with them. He will enjoin on them that which is right and forbid them that which is wrong. He will make lawful for them all good things and prohibit for them only the foul; and he will relieve them of their burden and the fetters that they used to wear. Then those who believe in him, and honor him, and help him, and follow the light which is sent down with him: they are the successful." (Quran 7:157)

Thus, the Quran confirms that the unlearned prophet foretold in the Bible was indeed Muhammad (peace be upon him). The stunningly precise prediction is further perceived from the following Hadeeth:

"The angel came to him and asked him to read. The Prophet replied, "I do not know how to read." (Hadeeth Sahih Bukhari 1:1:003)

In conclusion, it is evident that the Quran fills the void in the Bible, completing previous predictions.

(III.) Science

28. The Bible, the Quran, and Evolution

Errancy; God creates all life out of the waters (Genesis 1:20-21) *Vs* God creates all life out of the earth (Genesis 2:19)

Excuse; Mistranslation.

Rebuttal: (See Reply letter [I] in Rebuttal Chart)

Correction: Today, astronomers are equipped with powerful telescopes that can view the formation of our neighboring galaxies. From their studies, we have learned that galaxies are formed from the condensation of spiraling celestial "mists".

"Then He settled unto the firmament (sky) when it was smoke...." (Quran 41:11)

29. Chronological Inconsistency

Errancy; The Bible says that the earth was created in six days (Genesis 2:1) while modern scientists state that according to archeological evidence, the earth was created in a time span of millions of years.

Excuse; Mistranslation.

Rebuttal: (See Reply letter [I] in Rebuttal Chart)

Correction: The Quran is preserved and considered authentic in Arabic and thus the Arabic term in reference to the earth's creation is "periods" or "eons" rather than days as in Bible versions:

"Surely your Lord is Allah, Who created the heavens and the earth in six periods of time, and He is firm in power; He throws the veil of night over the day, which it pursues incessantly; and (He created) the sun and the moon and the stars, made subservient by His command; surely His is the creation and the command; blessed is Allah, the Lord of the worlds." (Quran 7:54)

30. Light in the Universe

Errancy; The Bible claims that there was light in the Universe on the first day of creation;

"And God said, "Let there be light"; and there was light. And God saw that the light was good; and God separated the light from the darkness. God called the light Day, and the darkness he called Night. And there was evening and there was morning, one day." (Genesis 1:3-5).

Yet, then we see in (Genesis 1:14), that the sun was not created until the fourth day. Without the sun, there is no light; hence, it is simply wrong to claim that there was light when the sun was not yet created.

Excuse; 1st) There are other sources of light in the Universe besides the sun. 2nd) The existent sun was blocked by clouds and was only able to appear on the fourth day.

Rebuttal: 1st) If there are other sources of light in the universe, then why is it dark at night when the sun sets? 2nd) God said in the Bible "Let there be lights in the firmament of the heaven" which is the queue phrase used by God pre-Creation. God did not say, "Let the clouds move out of the way".

Correction: We see this discrepancy is not in the Quran, as the Quran confirms what scientists of today agree upon, which is that the elements in the Universe were created at once, this is known as the "Big Bang theory"

As God, in the Quran, enlightens the writers of the Bible, there is no need to be confused in the matter of light in the Universe "Do not the disbelievers see that the heavens and the earth were fused then We ripped them asunder...." (Quran 21:30)

31. Growth of Plant Life

Errancy; Although, there are existing truths in the Bible, which come from God and have not been altered to this day, there are indeed other passages, which have obvious disagreements with scientifically known facts.

Another existing example presented is the growth of plant life on earth. According to the Bible, Formation of plant life began on the third day:

"And God said, "Let the earth put forth vegetation, plants yielding seed, and fruit trees bearing fruit in which is their seed, each according to its kind, upon the earth." And it was so." (Genesis 1:11)

The problem is that God created the Sun on the fourth day (Genesis 1:14) and complex seed formation cannot occur without sunlight.

Excuse; Mistranslation.

Rebuttal: (See Reply letter [I] in Rebuttal Chart)

Correction: The Quran clarifies that food appeared two eons after the light was in the Heavens:

"And He made in it mountains above its surface and He blessed therein and made therein its foods, in four periods: alike for the seekers." (Quran 41:10)

(Quran 41:11-12) use the adverbs (thummah and fa) which mean "a series of events." Neither of these two, however, is used in the 10th verse, which says four periods and uses the adverb (wa) meaning "parallel or overlapping" events.

Therefore, we see the total time to complete the mountain formation and food growth is four periods. Within two of these four periods, we see light:

"So He ordained them seven heavens in two periods, and revealed in every heaven its affair; and We adorned the lower heaven with brilliant stars and (made it) to guard; that is the decree of the Mighty, the Knowing." (Quran 41:12)

32. Animals created before man?

Errancy; Animals were created before man was created. (Genesis 1:24-27) *Vs* Man was created before animals were created. (Genesis 2:7, 19)

Excuse; (Genesis 2) is only descriptive and the two chapters do not exactly say when the animals were created.

Rebuttal: What apologetics fail to comprehend is that in (Genesis 1), after God made the animals, the decision to make man was consummated. While in (Genesis 2), after man was made, God said, "It is not good that the man should be alone," then the decision to make animals was executed.

Correction: Logically, animals were created before humans in order for humans to have food. The Holy Quran lists this sequence here:

"Hast thou not seen that unto Allah payeth adoration whosoever is in the heavens and whosoever is in the earth, and the sun, and the moon, and the stars, and the hills, and the trees, and the beasts, and many of mankind, while there are many unto whom the doom is justly due. He whom Allah scorneth, there is none to give him honor. Lo! Allah doeth what He will." (Quran 22:18)

33. Trees created before man

Errancy; Trees were created before man was created (Genesis 1:11-12, 26-27) *Vs* Man was created before trees were created. (Genesis 2:4-9)

Excuse; None available.

Correction: We see that the sequence is outlined correctly and without discrepancy in the Quran:

"Is not He (best) who created the heavens and the earth, and sendeth down for you water from the sky wherewith We cause to spring forth joyous orchards, whose trees it never hath been yours to cause to grow. Is there any God beside Allah? Nay, but they are folk who ascribe equals (unto Him)!" (Quran 27:60)

"Hast thou not seen that unto Allah payeth adoration whosoever is in the heavens and whosoever is in the earth, and the sun, and the moon, and the stars, and the hills, and the trees, and the beasts, and many of mankind, while there are many unto whom the doom is justly due. He whom Allah scorneth, there is none to give him honor. Lo! Allah doeth what He will." (Quran 22:18)

34. Why We Die

Errancy; In the Bible, Paul claims we die because of sin. Paul asserts that the first human sinned, therefore lost immortality, and subsequently caused all humans to be seemingly 'cursed' with death.

Paul blames Adam by saying ; "Wherefore, as by one man sin entered into the world, and death by sin; and so death passed upon all men, for that all have sinned" (Romans 5:12)

"For since by man came death, by man came also the resurrection of the dead. For as in Adam all die..." (1 Corinthians 15:21-22)

"Nevertheless death reigned from Adam to Moses, even over them that had not sinned..." (Romans 5:14)

"For the wages of sin is death....." (Romans 6:23)

"it is appointed for men to die once" (Hebrews 9:27)

Excuse; Jesus abolished death, but has not gotten the chance to actually do so yet.

Rebuttal: Either the claimed crucifixion had a great significance or not, either it removed death or not; which by the fact that we still must die, then the answer is that the supposed crucifixion had no significance.

If we had to wait until the second coming of Jesus, it would be too late; we would not know if Jesus did indeed remove death or not because it will be resurrection time.

Perhaps Paul did not know if Jesus removed death or not because he had not died yet.

Apparently Paul gained false confidence in defeating death by boldly preaching contradictory Gospels to both Jewish and Gentilian camps while briefly evading assassination, hence his false inspiration to make unfounded remarks regarding death.

Correction: Fortunately, today, scientists know that common death is caused by...Oxygen.

Oxygen is a natural element, which also helps in the corrosion of automobiles and flowers. The same reaction this element has towards metals and wild life, it too has towards our bodies, slowly aging us until death. This gas is a slow poison that affects each one differently as it also deteriorates metals and plants at various speeds.

As recommended by Doctors in the field of health and medicine, anti-Oxidants are shown to slow the aging process. Nonetheless, the anti-Oxidants do not stop our expiration date, and eventually, at a set time, we die.

The Holy Quran confirms this natural process and does not give us episodes of the 'original sin'. The Holy Quran gives us facts from our Creator that death is a normal process and we only live for a certain period and then return to God:

"And among His Signs in this: thou seest the earth barren and desolate; but when We send down rain to it, it is stirred to life and yields increase. Truly, He Who gives life to the (dead) earth can surely give life to (men) who are dead. For He has power over all things." (Quran 41:39)

"Lo! Allah (it is) Who splitteth the grain of corn and the date-stone (for sprouting); He brings forth the living from the dead and He is the bringer forth of the dead from the living; that is Allah! How are you then turned away." (Quran 6:95)

Nearly 1,400 years ago, prior to scientists confirming that the origin of death is the prolonged exposure to the elements on earth, the Holy Quran in these verses compares us to other living organisms. Summarizing that it is a common cycle for the earth to be barren, then brought back to life by the water descending from the Almighty God.

Therefore, the reason for death is not because of a sin or a curse, it is because of the environmental conditions of earth as stated in the Holy Quran. Roses are at one point in full bloom, and as the wilting process takes affect, the rose plant deteriorates and is eventually lifeless, the rose was not born a sinner as we are not born sinners.

This concrete evidence again shows that natural death is not a transmitted curse; instead, death is a natural geological process.

"Every soul shall have a taste of death: and We test you by evil and by good by way of trial. To Us must ye return." (Quran 21:35)

Signifying that death is universal, and no soul is exempt, the word "taste" here supports the fact that common death is due to our life term of inhaling oxygen-based gases.

"Yet have they taken, besides Him, gods that can create nothing but are themselves created; that have no control of hurt or good to themselves; nor can they control death nor life nor resurrection." (Quran 25:3)

It is precisely stated in this verse that neither humans nor created idols that are perceived as gods, can have any control over death, dying is an unavoidable necrosis and those who assumed human or petrified gods could make a human body immortal, were dead wrong .

The Quran debunks all fallacies of these ancient flesh god parables who give us immortality through sacrifices or ritual drinks, for dying is as an unavoidable occurrence as the sun setting is:

"And He it is Who gives life and causes death, and (in) His (control) is the alternation of the night and the day; do you not then understand?" (Quran 23:80)

The Divinity of this cycle is clear. If the sun did not set, and the night did not cover the land, then all of the earth would become barren, and with a constant sun 24 hours a day, the earth would wither away.

Similarly, if humans did not die, the resources on this earth would have been depleted. We are surrounded by cycles, within and without our Universe, we give birth, which maintains the existence of humans, so factually, both death and birth, maintains our presence here on earth.

Many cycles are referenced to within the Holy Quran which generates and preserves life on our planet, if any of the numerous sequences, including death, were removed from the repeated phenomenon's, the human race would fade away within a century.

If we observe our surroundings realistically, we need death and cannot exist without it. Life and death are as perfect a pair as day and night:

"And all things We have created by pairs, that haply ye may reflect." (Quran 51:49)

Death in Islam is a transitional process; to die is nothing to remorse about:

"Think not of those who are slain in Allah's way as dead. Nay, they live, finding their sustenance in the presence of their Lord" (Quran 3:169)

In conclusion, both the Quran and science do not scapegoat death and instead explain it as a natural cycle.

35. Shape of Earth

Errancy; Despite the 180-Degree shift by modern Biblical apologetics in comparison to the previous 15 centuries of Christian scholars, we are still left with passages in the Bible, which strongly indicate the earth is flat;

"And he shall set up an ensign for the nations, and shall assemble the outcasts of Israel, and gather together the dispersed of Judah from the four corners of the earth" (Isaiah 11:12)

"that it might take the earth by the edges and shake the wicked out of it" (Job 38:13)"

"And after these things I saw four angels standing on four corners of the earth, holding the four winds of the earth, that the wind should not blow on the earth, nor on the sea, nor on any tree." (Revelation 7:1)

"The tree grew, and was strong, and the height thereof reached unto heaven, and the sight thereof to the ends of all the earth" (Daniel 4:11)

"Again, the devil taketh him up into an exceeding high mountain, and sheweth him all the kingdoms of the world, and the glory of them" (Matthew 4:8)

These passages clearly indicated that the earth has four corners and that the entire earth could be seen from one end to the other. Modern day Bible followers may not interpret those passages as such, but centuries of Christian scholars beforehand did just that. The centuries of Christian scholars who support the flat earth belief are;

Lactantius (AD 245–325), a professional rhetorician who converted to Christianity mid-life.

Severian of Gabala (380).

Cosmas Indicopleustes, sixth century Eastern Greek Christian who claimed the Earth was flat and lay beneath the heavens (consisting of a rectangular vaulted arch).

In the books, "Tremendous Treks" by Peter Kent and "Christopher Columbus" by Lucio Sorre, the popular Christian attitude of the earth being flat are well documented amongst the masses.

Excuse; That's what is says but that's not what it means, the four corners are actually references to north, south, east and west.

Rebuttal: (See Reply letter [E] in Rebuttal Chart) It is unacceptable to claim that the four corners were referring to navigational directions for three obvious reasons. The first is that when the Bible depicts navigational directions, then it actually says those directions and not the square description of "four corners of the earth."

"And thy seed shall be as the dust of the earth, and thou shalt spread abroad to the west, and to the east, and to the north, and to the south: and in thee and in thy seed shall all the families of the earth be blessed." (Genesis 28:14)

The second reason why the apologetics attempt to change the meaning of "four corners" fails is that the term "four corners" is used elsewhere to mean a square structure;

"And, behold, there came a great wind from the wilderness, and smote the four corners of the house, and it fell upon the young men, and they are dead; and I only am escaped alone to tell thee." (Job 1:19)

The third reason is that the Bible writers state that they can see all four corners of the earth;

"And after these things I saw four angels standing on the four corners of the earth" (Revelation 7:1)

Hence, confirming this earth is flat because if you can see all four corners of your house, then you are standing on a flat ground.

Correction: The Quran clearly and consistently states the shape of the earth is spherical:

"…and the earth, after that, He (God) made it 'dahaha' (oval shape)" (Quran 79:30)

36. <u>Earth Moving?</u>

Errancy; The reason why the notion that the earth was the center of the Universe up until 1,600 AD, was so popular amongst the masses and the church was because of the Bible's claim that the earth was motionless, and instead, other celestial objects circled the earth;

"The Lord is king. He is clothed with majesty and strength. The earth is set firmly in place and cannot be moved." (Psalms 93:1)

"Say among the nations, "The Lord reigns." The world is firmly established, it cannot be moved; he will judge the peoples with equity." (Psalms 96:10)

"Who laid the foundations of the earth, that it should not be removed for ever." (Psalms 104:5)

"tremble before him, all the earth; yea, the world stands firm, never to be moved." (1 Chronicles 16:30)

To dispel any doubts about the "Planet" earth being motionless, the Hebrew word for "earth" was found to be "erets" which means;

"whole earth (as opposed to a part) and earth (as opposed to heaven)" *The KJV Old Testament Hebrew Lexicon.*

Excuse; This passage is taken literally instead of symbolically or metaphorically.

Rebuttal: (See Reply letter [H] in Rebuttal Chart)

Correction: The Holy Quran shows that the earth is not a motionless body, and instead, the earth orbits other celestial bodies:

"It is He Who created the night and the day, and the sun and the moon: all (the celestial bodies) swim along, each in its rounded course." (Quran 21:33)

37. Earth Supported

Errancy; The earth has no foundation (Job 26:7) *Vs* Earth sits upon pillars (1 Samuel 2:8, Job 9:6)

Excuse; That is what it says but that is not what it means; When God says "earth pillars," He means fixtures such as mountains.

Rebuttal: (See Reply letter [E] in Rebuttal Chart) This excuse would be valid except for what (1 Samuel 2:8) states; "for the pillars of the earth are the Lord's, and he hath set the world upon them."

Since the earth is not placed on top of the mountains, we are forced to conclude that the Bible is speaking of the pillars beneath the earth, not the ones on the earth.

Correction: The Holy Quran settles the contradiction of whether there are or are not pillars supporting the earth by stating:

"God it is Who raised up the heavenly bodies to invisible pillars and then took repose on the throne..." (Quran 13:2)

In conclusion, there are pillars, only they cannot be seen as the Quran clarifies.

38. Heaven Supported

Errancy; Columns or Pillars are supporting Heaven;

"The pillars of heaven tremble, and are astonished at his reproof." (Job 26:11)

Yet when astronauts traveled through space, no pillars were visible.

Excuse; That is what it says but that is not what it means.

Rebuttal: (See Reply letter [E] in Rebuttal Chart)

Correction: The Holy Quran confirms what astronauts have discovered, nearly 1,400 years before they saw there were no visible pillars as the Bible describes. Once again, the Quran erases an errancy:

"He hath created the heavens without supports that ye can see, and hath cast into the earth firm mountains, so that it quake not with you; and He hath dispersed therein all kinds of beasts. And We send down water from the sky and We cause (plants) of every goodly kind to grow therein." (Quran 31:10)

39. Life Span?

Errancy; The Bible gives contradictory life span limits which are absent from the Quran;

We will live up to 120 years = "Then the Lord said, "My Spirit shall not strive with man forever, because he also is flesh; nevertheless his days shall be one hundred and twenty years." (Genesis 6:3)

We will live up to 101 years = "No longer will there be in it an infant (who lives but a few) days, Or an old man who does not live out his days; For the youth will die at the age of one hundred And the one who does not reach the age of one hundred Will be (thought) accursed." (Isaiah 65:20)

We will live up to 80 years = "As for the days of our life, they contain seventy years, Or if due to strength, eighty years, Yet their pride is (but) labor and sorrow; For soon it is gone and we fly away." (Psalms 90:10)

Although all three life spans differ from each other, the sharpest inconsistency is between (Psalms 90:10) where with strength, we will live up to 80 and (Isaiah 65:20) if anyone does not live up to 100 is accursed. Therefore, according to the Bible's own life expectancy, the majority of humans will be cursed because most of us do not reach 100.

Excuse; Longevity decreased over time as a curse from God (Genesis 6:3)

Rebuttal: First, Jesus in the Bible supposedly removed all past sins over 2,000 years ago, yet most humans still barely reach 100. Second, the supposed curse from God was that our life span decreases from 900 to 120, yet rarely any of us still reach 120. Third, this curse excuse is invalid because many people (since the supposed curse was ordained) had surpassed the assumed cursed year. Further evaluation reveals that various humans broke the life span set in the Bible;

Noah, nine-hundred and fifty years (Genesis 9:29)
Shem, six-hundred years (Genesis 11:10-11)
Arphaxad, four-hundred and thirty-eight years (Genesis 11:12-13)
Salah, four-hundred and thirty-three years (Genesis 11:14-15)
Eber, four-hundred and sixty-four years (Genesis 11:16-17)
Peleg, two-hundred and thirty-nine years (Genesis 11:18-19)
Reu, two-hundred and thirty-nine years (Genesis 11:20-21)
Serug, two-hundred and thirty years (Genesis 11:22-23)
Terah, two-hundred and five years (Genesis 11:32)
Isaac, one-hundred and eighty years (Genesis 35:28)
Abraham, one-hundred and seventy-five years (Genesis 25:7)
Nahor, one-hundred and forty-eight years (Genesis 11:24-25)
Jacob, one-hundred and forty-seven years (Genesis 47:28)
Job, one-hundred and forty years (Job 42:16-17)
Amram, one-hundred and thirty-seven years (Exodus 6:20)
Jehoiada, one-hundred and thirty years (2 Chronicles 24:15)
Sarah, one-hundred and twenty-seven years (Genesis 23:1)

Therefore, longevity did not decrease as apologetics claim, it was sporadic, in fact, according to today's scientists, with the discoveries of various cures, our longevity is increasing.

Correction: The Quran corrects the scrambled life spans portrayed in the Bible by simply stating;

"Allah gives life and takes life away." (Quran 3:156)

"When their time comes they will not be an hour late or an hour early." (Quran 7:34)

"Nor take life - which Allah has made sacred - except for just cause. And if anyone is slain wrongfully, we have given his heir authority (to demand qisas or to forgive): but let him not exceed bounds in the matter of taking life; for he is helped (by the Law)." (Quran 17.033)

"And a soul will not die but with the permission of Allah the term is fixed"; (Quran 3:145)

"We have ordained death among you and We are not to be outrun" (Quran 56:60)

Therefore, we realize from the Quran; which is free from inconsistent life expectancies as asserted in the Bible, that God controls longevity. Death is not a curse; it is a natural human condition, which can happen at anytime. Hence, it is critical to worship God everyday, and not expect to wait 120 years to meet our Maker.

40. On Earth Forever?

Errancy; The earth will last for ever (Ecclesiastes 1:4) *Vs* The earth will be destroyed (2 Peter 3:10)

Excuse; Mistranslation.

Rebuttal: (See Reply letter [I] in Rebuttal Chart)

Correction: The life of this world is short if we all but knew how short;

"On the day when the earth will be changed to other than the earth, and the heavens (also will be changed) and they (humans) will come forth unto Allah, the One, the Almighty" (Quran 14:48)

41. Seeking Knowledge

Errancy; The joy of wisdom (Proverbs 3:13-15) *Vs* The misery of wisdom (Ecclesiastes 1:18)

Excuse; Solomon is seeking earthly wisdom, instead of Godly wisdom.

Rebuttal: Everything below and above the sun is made by God and achieving wisdom through learning is a holy act.

Correction: The Quran consistently teaches us that seeking wisdom is the key to happiness:

"Those who seek and acquire knowledge are a step closer to righteousness than those without the knowledge to do the righteous actions. But those of them who are firm in knowledge and the believers believe in that which is revealed unto thee, and that which was revealed before thee, especially the diligent in prayer and those who pay the poor due, the believers in Allah and the Last Day. Upon these We shall bestow immense reward." (Quran 4:162)

42. Examining Embryology

Errancy; In examining embryology in the Bible, we discover discrepancies in relation to modern scientific knowledge. We also find a stunning similarity to ancient Greek theorists on embryology.

"Remember, I beseech thee, that thou hast fashioned me as clay; and wilt thou bring me into the dust again! Hast thou not poured me out as milk, and curdled me like cheese? Thou hast clothed me with skin and flesh, and knit me together with bones and sinews." (Job 10:9-11)

The comparison of embryology with the making of cheese is strikingly identical to a comparison the ancient Greek philosopher Aristotle makes in his book *On the Generation of Animals* (pg. 64-65)

Furthermore, the notion of being sewn together within the womb appears to be an ongoing theme;

"For You created my innermost being; You knit me together in my mother's womb. I praise You because I am fearfully and wonderfully made." (Psalms 139:13-14)

Excuse; Mistranslation.

Rebuttal: (See Reply letter [I] in Rebuttal Chart)

Correction: These Biblical inconsistencies are corrected by the explanation of embryology in the Quran:

"He makes you in the wombs of your mothers in stages, one after another, in three veils of darkness." (Quran 39:6)

"Then We placed him as a drop in a place of rest." (Quran 23:13)

"Then of that leech-like structure, We made a chewed lump. Then We made out of the chewed lump, bones, and clothed the bones in flesh." (Quran 23:14)

Verse 23:14 indicates that at the chewed lump stage, bones and muscles form. This is in accordance with scientific findings. First, the cartilage forms, then the muscles and flesh develop around them from the somatic mesoderm.

This corrects the Bible's assertion that the skin is made first and then "knitted" onto the bones (Job 10:10). The Quran also debunks any fallacies that we are poured like milk and that amount of milk is made into an equal amount cheese. Instead, we are created from a drop, which grows in stages. As we know, when milk is poured, it "shrinks" into cheese. The Bible describes an opposite embryology process from that which is proven by modern scientists and confirmed in the Quran; a drop is "expanding" into the newborn.

According to Keith L. Moore, PhD, Professor of Anatomy and Associate Dean Basic Sciences, Faculty of Medicine, at the University of Toronto;

"For the past three years, I have worked with the Embryology Committee of King Abdulaziz University in Jeddah, Saudi Arabia, helping them to interpret the many statements in the Quran and the Sunnah referring to human reproduction and prenatal development. At first I was astonished by the accuracy of the statements that were recorded in the seventh century AD, before the science of embryology was established."

The Quran has revealed the process of birth centuries before modern x-ray machines could validate it, hence proving its Divinity and correcting the embryology process that is falsely described in the Bible.

43. From the Bowels?

Errancy; The Bible claims that children come from the bowels;

"By thee have I been holden up from the womb: thou art he that took me out of my mother's bowels: my praise shall be continually of thee." (Psalms 71:6)

"Listen, O isles, unto me; and hearken, ye people, from far; The Lord hath called me from the womb; from the bowels of my mother hath he made mention of my name." (Isaiah 49:1)

Only one out of ten thousand pregnancies does a baby develop in the mother's bowel. This is known as an abdominal ectopic pregnancy and in 95 percent of these cases, the baby dies before birth.

Excuse; None available.

Correction: God corrects this horrific thought of babies being born from the bowels as noted in the Bible:

"And Allah brought you forth from the wombs of your mothers knowing nothing, and gave you hearing and sight and hearts that haply ye might give thanks." (Quran 16:78)

"Allah knoweth that which every female beareth and that which the wombs absorb and that which they grow. And everything with Him is measured." (Quran 13:8)

(IV.) LAWS

44. Covet Gifts?

Errancy; Do not covet worldly material (Exodus 20:17) *Vs* Covet worldly material. (1 Corinthians 12:31)

Excuse; That is what it says but that is not what it means. In (1 Corinthians 12:31), covet means desire lawfully.

Rebuttal: (See Reply letter [E] in Rebuttal Chart). Any envy is evil in the Bible (Proverbs 14:30). Second, (Exodus 20:17) does not differentiate between lawful or unlawful coveting. Lastly, worldly temptation in the Bible only comes from the devil, thus always unlawful;

"Let no one say when he is tempted, "I am being tempted by God"; for God cannot be tempted by evil, and He Himself does not tempt anyone. But each one is tempted when he is carried away and enticed by his own lust." (James 1:13-14)

Correction: The Quran corrects the Bible by consistently specifying that coveting is a sin:

"And covet not the thing in which Allah hath made some of you excel others. Unto men a fortune from that which they have earned, and unto women a fortune from that which they have earned. (Envy not one another) but ask Allah of His bounty. Lo! Allah is ever Knower of all things." (Quran 4:32)

45. The Forgiving Cow?

Errancy; A cow can be used to forgive murder (Deuteronomy 21:1-9) *Vs* A cow cannot be used to forgive a murder (Numbers 35:33, Psalms 49:7)

In (Deuteronomy 21:1-9), the Bible records that Jews were forgiven for murdering an innocent man by simply killing a cow. This is truly a degradation of human life and what is even a more disturbing thought is that the Bible editors may have been motivated to record the story in this manner in order to alleviate the guilt off the Jewish people. This Biblical story is also in line with how the Jews from Ancient Egypt thought the cow was sacred and in this case, equal to the murdering of a human life.

Excuse; None available.

Correction: The Holy Quran clarifies this account with righteous accurateness. The Quran preserves the preciousness of human life and shows God as a Righteous Judge for our affairs. In the Quran, the cow was used to reveal the hidden murderer and not used to actually be an atonement the murderer:

"Remember ye slew a man and fell into a dispute among yourselves as to the crime: But Allah was to bring forth what ye did hide. So We said: Strike the (dead body) with part of the (Sacrificed cow), thus Allah brings the dead to life, and He shows you His signs so that you may understand." (Quran 2:72-73)

Thus showing the murderer cannot hide because God knows all and can bring the dead back to life on earth to reveal their attackers, and simultaneously correcting the notion that a cow can be used as an expiation for a murder.

46. Celibacy Preferred?

Errancy; Marriage encouraged (Genesis 2:18-24, 1 Timothy 4:1- 5) *Vs* Marriage discouraged (1 Corinthians 7:8)

Excuse; That is what it says but that is not what it means. Paul is not saying, "don't get married"; he is merely stating, "it's better not to be married."

Rebuttal: First, this adds to the contradiction because God in the Bible says it is better to be married;

"Then the Lord God said, "It is not good for the man to live alone. I will make a suitable companion to help him." (Genesis 2:18)

Secondly, further down in (1st Corinthians), Paul reiterates himself by telling the single people not to get married;

"Are you unmarried? Then don't look for a wife." (1 Corinthians 7:27)

This commandment by Paul in the Bible has been followed to the letter by Christian Priests world wide, forsaking marriage for a life of celibacy. This proves that Paul is not merely making a suggestion, but instead creating a conflicting law.

Correction: Islam agrees with human nature. Islam is well known as the "natural religion" for Islam is in harmony with a human's body, mind, and soul. The Quran teaches us to:

"Marry those among you who are single, or the virtuous ones among yourselves, male or female: if they are in poverty, Allah will give them means out of His grace: for Allah encompasseth all, and he knoweth all things." (Quran 24:32)

"This day are (all) things good and pure made lawful unto you. The food of the People of the Book is lawful unto you and yours is lawful unto them. (Lawful unto you in marriage) are (not only) chaste women who are believers, but chaste women among the People of the Book, revealed before your time, - when ye give them their due dowers, and desire chastity, not lewdness, nor secret intrigues if any one rejects faith, fruitless is his work, and in the Hereafter he will be in the ranks of those who have lost (all spiritual good)." (Quran 5:5)

In conclusion, the hierarchies in the Christian religion such as Priests and Nuns, in violation of nature, do not marry. While all Muslims including Sheikhs, Imams, Muftis, and Ministers are encouraged to marry. Islam agrees with how God fashioned us.

47. Halal is Kosher

Errancy; The Bible states that some laws were given as a form of punishment because of disobedience;

"Because they had not executed my judgments, but had despised my statutes, and had polluted my sabbaths, and their eyes were after their fathers' idols. Wherefore I gave them also laws that were not good, and judgments whereby they should not live; And I polluted them in their own gifts, in that they caused to pass through the fire all that openeth the womb, that I might make them desolate, to the end that they might know that I am the Lord." (Ezekiel 20:24-26)

When we analyze the Bible, we discover that some dietary laws fit into the category of "bad laws" given to make certain folk desolate. For example, we know that with desert people, starvation was very common and certain foods being forbidden to them meant death.

With the Monotheist's health and wellness being a priority, nutritional foods which were previously forbidden in the Bible such as shrimp, rabbit, (parts of a camel), sea food such as lobster and shell fish in proportion, are allowed in the Quran;

"Nevertheless these ye shall not eat of them that chew the cud, or of them that divide the cloven hoof; as the camel, and the hare, and the coney: for they chew the cud, but divide not the hoof; therefore they are unclean unto you." (Deuteronomy 14:7)

"These ye shall eat of all that are in the waters: all that have fins and scales shall ye eat: And whatsoever hath not fins and scales ye may not eat; it is unclean unto you." (Deuteronomy 14:9-10)

Excuse; None available.

Correction: We find that the foods that have been forbidden in the Bible yet allowed in the Quran are the ones that do not cause harm or illness according to medical tests. Health is one of the central themes in the Quran.

"(And it is said unto them): Eat and drink in health (as a reward) for what ye used to do" (Quran 52:19)

God sent the Holy Quran as a mercy to humans, God reminds us in the Quran of the (Ezekiel 20:24) event;

"And to those who were Jews We made unlawful every animal with undivided hoof, and of oxen and sheep We made unlawful to them the fat of both, except such as was on their backs or the entrails or what was mixed with bones: this was a punishment We gave them on account of their rebellion, and We are surely Truthful." (Quran 6:146) see also (Quran 3:93 and 4:160).

Such a restriction in the desert of Israel and Arabia would surely kill the follower through starvation and make the number of followers small in population, as God had promised to make Israelites desolate.

For example, God forbade both nutritional and non-nutritional foods for the Israelites while forgiving those who repented and returned to Allah. To the best of our modern scientific knowledge, there is no reason why rabbit or camel meat is any less healthy than cow or goat meat. With the scarcity of food in the desert, being forbidden from eating healthy meat meant death. Therefore, God sent down the forgiving message in the Holy Quran, for the Israelites who repented, their dietary laws were kept kosher, but with mercy rather than a curse:

"We send down (stage by stage) in the Quran that which is a healing and a mercy to those who believe: to the unjust it causes nothing but loss after loss." (Quran 17:82)

"…This (Quran) is insight from your Lord, and a guidance and a mercy for a people that believe." (Quran 7:204)

An example of this dietary mercy is recorded in the Quran:

"The sacrificial camels we have made for you as among the symbols from Allah: in them is (much) good for you: then pronounce the name of Allah over them as they line up (for sacrifice): when they are down on their sides (after slaughter), eat ye thereof, and feed such as (beg not but) live in contentment, and such as beg with due humility: thus have We made animals subject to you, that ye may be grateful." (Quran 22:36)

God reveals in this verse that camels actually are nutritional, whereas in the Torah they were forbidden not because of health reasons like pork, but because of disobedience of Israelites. God also explains that we were mercifully allowed to eat previously forbidden meats so that we can be content and not beg.

Rather than begging for food or starving to death due to a Biblical law placed on ancient Israelites because of an ancient act of disobedience, today's Monotheists are forgiven and allowed to eat all healthy foods while still being restricted from only those foods which are deemed unhealthy for the body.

48. Vegetarian?

Errancy; Eat only vegetables (Genesis 1:29-30) *Vs* Eat everything [Meats and Vegetables] (Genesis 9:3)

Excuse; Later commandments supersede the previous ones.

Rebuttal: This would be acceptable except for the fact that later commandments continued to supersede previous ones in the Bible;

"It is right not to eat meat - or to do anything else that will cause your brother to fall" (Romans 14:21).

Correction: The Quran is free from inconsistencies as we are always taught that both meats and vegetables are lawful for us with the exception of meat that can harm our well-being, such as swine meat:

"He has only forbidden you dead meat, and blood, and the flesh of swine, and any (food) over which the name of other than Allah has been invoked. But if one is forced by necessity, without willful disobedience, nor transgressing due limits, then Allah is Oft Forgiving, Most Merciful." (Quran 16:115)

49. Sabbath Reason

Errancy; Sabbath kept because God rested on the seventh day after creating the universe (Exodus 20:11) *Vs* Sabbath kept because God delivered the Israelites from Egypt (Deuteronomy 5:15)

"Remember that you were slaves in Egypt, and that I, the Lord your God, rescued you by my great power and strength. That is why I command you to observe the Sabbath."

Excuse; Both passages are complimenting each other; there can be multiple reasons to obey a particular law.

Rebuttal: It would be sufficient for humans to keep the Sabbath as gratitude to God for creating the Universe. It would be beneath God to continually try to coax humans to keep the Sabbath, namely for helping them escape from Egypt.

Second, (Deuteronomy 5:15) is speaking of a singular reason, not multiple reasons;

"Remember that you were slaves in Egypt, and that I, the Lord your God, rescued you by my great power and strength. That is why I command you to observe the Sabbath." (Deuteronomy 5:15)

God does not say "that is –one of the reasons- why I command you to observe the Sabbath."

Third, there is no proof that Adam and Eve along with all the Prophets prior to Moses ever kept or observed the Sabbath, indicating (Deuteronomy 5:15) was when it first became a Law.

Correction: The Holy Quran corrects multiple misconceptions in this account. (Quran 50:38) clarifies that:

1) The universe was not created in 6 days, but rather 6 periods, so the day as a whole does not bare chronological significance.

2) God never gets tired, thus never rests, therefore we are not to rest on that day.

3) The Sabbath is a period for remembrance, not rest, thus removing the constraining curse of not working that entire day. (Continued from 49 to 50)

50. <u>Work on the Sabbath?</u>

Errancy; Do not work on the Sabbath (Exodus 31:15) *Vs* Prophet Jesus worked on the Sabbath (John 5:16, Matthew 12:1-3, 5)

Excuse; Jesus was God, thus he was allowed to break the Sabbath

Rebuttal: If Jesus were the God of the Bible, why would he break a law he specified for resting?

Correction: The Holy Quran as a completion of the Bible explains that Jesus was emphasizing the point that the Sabbath was about remembrance, not work.

Jesus declared that God never stops working, even on the Sabbath day (John 5:16) which is correctly confirmed in the (Quran 2:255)

Not working on Sabbath was a judgment placed on rebellious Israelites who considered the new law a curse, because God never rests, the financial restraint put on the Israelites was instead a punishment as perceived in the Bible;

"When will the new moon be gone, that we may sell corn? and the Sabbath, that we may set forth wheat, making the ephah small, and the shekel great, and falsifying the balances by deceit? That we may buy the poor for silver, and the needy for a pair of shoes; yea, and sell the refuse of the wheat?" (Amos 8:4-6)

"Men of Tyre also, who lived in the city, brought in fish and all kinds of wares and sold them on the Sabbath to the people of Judah, and in Jerusalem." (Nehemiah 13:16)

The Sabbath that was issued to the rebellious Hebrews with Moses became an unbearable restraint towards the Bounties of God to the Israelites, then starting with Jesus as a righteous messenger of God and completed with God's reiteration in the Holy Quran, the obedient were forgiven.

Thus, the Holy Quran explains that the Sabbath is a day of remembrance, rather than rest. The merciful removal of the restriction from God's bounty is specified in the following verses:

"O ye who believe! When the call is proclaimed to prayer on Friday (the Day of Assembly), hasten earnestly to the Remembrance of Allah, and leave off business (and traffic): That is best for you if ye but knew! "And when the Prayer is finished, then may ye disperse through the land, and seek of the Bounty of Allah: and celebrate the Praises of Allah often (and without stint): that ye may prosper." "(Quran 62:9-10)

The curse of financial confinement is forgivingly removed in the Quran while the substance and content of the Sabbath is in place.

51. Freeing Slaves

Errancy; Slavery not allowed (Isaiah 58:6) *Vs* Slavery allowed (Exodus 21:7-8, Ephesians 6:5, Colossians 3:22)

Excuse; (Isaiah 58:6) does not forbid all slavery, and Paul is just commenting on a condition of his days, which is Semitic slavery, thus saying, "be good employees"

Rebuttal: By trying to correct the contradiction, the Biblicists confirm the evils of slave promotion in the Bible, which have been used to justify slavery for centuries towards Semitics and Gentiles alike.

Correction: The Holy Quran tells us not to enslave other humans:

"It is not (possible) for any human being unto whom Allah had given the Scripture and wisdom and the prophethood that he should afterwards have said unto mankind: Be slaves of me instead of Allah; but (what he said was): Be ye faithful servants of the Lord by virtue of your constant teaching of the Scripture and of your constant study thereof." (Quran 3:79)

Besides not enslaving fellow humans, the Holy Quran teaches us to free existing slaves:

"And let those who do not find the means to marry keep themselves chaste, till Allah gives them independence by His grace. And if any of your slaves ask for a deed in writing (of emancipation), give them such a deed if ye know any good in them: yea, give them something yourselves out of the means which Allah has given to you. - Oft-Forgiving, Most Merciful" (Quran 24:33)

52. <u>Good Laws?</u>

Errancy; The Laws are delightful (Psalms 119:35) *Vs* The Laws are a curse (Galatians 3:10-13)

Excuse; The laws were good to follow until the resurrection. After the resurrection, the laws were done away with;

"Purge out therefore the old leaven, that ye may be a new lump, as ye are unleavened. For even Christ our Passover is sacrificed for us" (1 Corinthians 5:7)

Rebuttal: It is a faulty notion to claim the laws, which were followed for millenniums, were only made to be temporary. Both the God of Abraham and Jesus state the laws are forever;

"Everlasting" ,"For All Generations", "a Perpetual Ordinance " (Exodus 27:21; 28:43; 29:28; 30:21; 31:17; Leviticus 6:18, 22; 7:34, 36; 10:9, 15; 17:7; 23:14, 21, 41; 24:3; Numbers 10:8; 15:15; 18:8, 11, 19, 23; 19:10; Deuteronomy 5:29; Psalms 119:160) and is Not to be changed or taken away from (Deuteronomy 4:2; 12:32).

Jesus confirms the Laws are for all generations and everlasting by following the laws (Matthew 8:4, 26:19, John 7:10).

Actions speak louder than words and besides the actions of Jesus keeping the Everlasting Laws, Jesus also states;

"Think not that I am come to destroy the law, or the prophets: I am not come to destroy, but to fulfill. For verily I say unto you, Till heaven and earth pass, one jot or one title shall in no wise pass from the law, till all be fulfilled." (Matthew 5:17-18)

In conclusion, the God of Abraham, the Prophets, and the Messiah all say the Laws are unending. The Righteous have one Enemy, he who leads people astray through lethargy.

Correction: God, through the Holy Quran explains that it is a combination of Faith and Works that gives us Salvation:

"For Him (alone) is prayer in Truth: any others that they call upon besides Him hear them no more than if they were to stretch forth their hands for water to reach their mouths but it reaches them not: for the prayer of those without Faith is nothing but (futile) wandering (in the mind)." (Quran 13:14)

The Holy Quran explains that works are to our benefit:

"O you whose hearts have been touched with the divine hand: When you intend to stand before God for performing your act of worship, then ablution becomes a duty. Wash your faces, your hands and the forearms up to the elbows, and with your wet hands wipe your heads, then wash your feet to the ankles....- God does not intend to put you in difficulty but only to make you sound headed men of proper discipline and excellent mind, and to set you upon a course of purity of thought and action, for the actions of men are best interpreters of their thoughts, and He means to make all grace abound in you that you may hopefully actuate yourselves with the feeling of gratitude and gratefulness and lift Him your inward sight." (Quran 5:6)

The Holy Quran teaches us that Jesus only came to clarify the previous scripture, not to change it, and he came to promote the most important law, to worship our Creator:

"When Jesus came with clear proofs (of Allah's Sovereignty), he said: I have come unto you with wisdom, and to make plain some of that concerning which ye differ. So keep your duty to Allah, and obey me."

"For Allah, He is my Lord and your Lord: so worship ye Him: this is a Straight Way." (Quran 43:63-64)

53. Poor or Preachers?

Errancy; There is some discord in the Bible regarding who is to receive tithes;

When a rich man asked Jesus, Jesus replied;

"If thou wilt be perfect, go and sell that thou hast, and -give to the poor-, and thou shalt have treasure in heaven" (Matthew 19:21)

Also;

"At the end of every third year you shall bring out all the tithe of your produce in that year, and shall deposit it in your town. And the Levite, because he has no portion or inheritance among you, and the alien, the orphan and the widow who are in your town, shall come and eat and be satisfied, in order that the Lord your God may bless you in all the work of your hand which you do (Deuteronomy 14:28-29).

Tithes went to the poor, the widows, and the orphans. Yet, In the Gospel, Paul claims that he should take the tithes;

"In the same way the Lord has given orders that those who preach the Gospel should be supported by those who accept it." (1 Corinthians 9:14)

This is a false claim by Paul, for no where in the Bible does Jesus or God command to give money to those who preach the Gospel, though unfortunately it seems that the Church follows Paul more than God.

Excuse; Paul was saying he would take the money to redistribute it to the poor.

Rebuttal: Paul is clearly saying that those who preach should get paid for it. Furthermore, Jesus never said, "give me the money to redistribute to the poor." Instead, Jesus taught people to give directly to the poor as Muslims do.

Correction: Islam corrects these man-inserted laws in the Bible;

"(Charity is) for those in need, who, in Allah's cause are restricted (from travel), and cannot move about in the land, seeking (For trade or work): the ignorant man thinks, because of their modesty, that they are free from want. Thou shalt know them by their (Unfailing) mark: They beg not importunately from all the sundry. And whatever of good ye give, be assured Allah knoweth it well." (Quran 2:273)

"They give food, out of love for Him (Allah), to the poor, the orphan, and the slave, saying: We feed you only for Allah's pleasure - we desire from you neither reward nor thanks." (Quran 76:8-9)

The difference between the Church and Islamic charity is that large amounts of money are left with individuals in the Church, therefore opening the opportunity for corruption, while in Islam, most of the charity goes directly to the poor.

54. Charge Interest?

Errancy; Do not charge interest to anyone (Deuteronomy 23:19) *Vs* Charge interest to all except the poor (Exodus 22:25)

Excuse; It may have been hard to distinguish who was poor and the law was later revised to include everyone.

Rebuttal: The Bible gives specific details as to who qualifies as a poor person regarding interest;

"If anyone from your country becomes too poor to support himself, help him to live among you as you would a stranger or foreigner. Do not charge him any interest on money you loan to him, but respect your God; let the poor live among you. Don't lend him money for interest, and don't try to make a profit from the food he buys." (Leviticus 25:35-37)

Hence, this excuse is disqualified from being valid.

Correction: The Holy Quran correcting the discrepancies in the Bible teaches us that usury is to be forbidden on all people whether it is for the taking or giving of usury:

"Allah does not bless usury, and He causes charitable deeds to prosper, and Allah does not love any ungrateful sinner." (Quran 2:276)

"O ye who believe! Observe your duty to Allah, and give up what remaineth (due to you) from usury, if ye are (in truth) believers." (Quran 2:278)

"They (people of the Book) took usury, though they were forbidden; and that they devoured men's substance wrongfully; - we have prepared for those among them who reject faith a grievous punishment." (Quran 4:161)

"That which ye lay out for increase through the property of (other) people, will have no increase with Allah: but that which ye lay out for charity, seeking the Countenance of Allah, (will increase): it is these who will get a recompense multiplied." (Quran 30:39)

55. Bribery Encouraged?

Errancy; The Bible promotes bribery;

"I tell you, make friends for yourselves using worldly riches so that when those riches are gone, you will be welcomed in those homes that continue forever." (Luke 16:9) *Vs* "You shall not take a bribe, for a bribe blinds the clear-sighted and subverts the cause of the just." (Exodus 23:8)

Excuse; None available.

Correction: Bribery is forbidden in all circumstances as recorded in the Quran:

"And do not eat up your property among yourselves for vanities, nor use it as bait for the judges, with intent that ye may eat up wrongfully and knowingly a little of (other) people's property." (Quran 2:188)

56. To Fast

Errancy; Fasting is for three weeks (Daniel 10:2-3) *Vs* Fasting is for forty days (Deuteronomy 9:9-18, Matthew 4:1-2)

There is no consistent standard or time frame taught in the Bible. It is obvious that many of the Prophets in the Bible fasted, hence we must "be like them" but no clear guidance is within the Bible as to how long to fast.

Excuse; None available.

Correction: Unlike the Bible, the Holy Quran specifies the period for fasting as being one month:

"Ramadan is the (month) in which was sent down the Quran, as a guide to mankind, also clear (Signs) for guidance and judgment (Between right and wrong). So every one of you who is present (at his home) during that month should spend it in fasting, but if any one is ill, or on a journey, the prescribed period (Should be made up) by days later. Allah intends every facility for you; He does not want to put to difficulties. (He wants you) to complete the prescribed period, and to glorify Him in that He has guided you; and perchance ye shall be grateful." (Quran 2:185)

Thus, the Holy Quran clarifies the standard date, time, reason, and method of fasting, unlike the Bible.

57. The Fate of apostates

Errancy; The Bible claims that if someone turns away from God, they are lost forever and to be killed;

"For how can those who abandon their faith be brought back to repent again? They were once in God's light; they tasted heaven's gift and received their share of the Holy Spirit; they knew from experience that God's word is good, and they had felt the powers of the coming age. And then they abandoned their faith! It is impossible to bring them back to repent again, because they are again crucifying the Son of God and exposing him to public shame." (Hebrews 6:4-6)

And

"But when the righteous turneth away from his righteousness, and committeth iniquity, and doeth according to all the abominations that the wicked man doeth, shall he live? All his righteousness that he hath done shall not be mentioned: in his trespass that he hath trespassed, and in his sin that he hath sinned, in them shall he die." (Ezekiel 18:24)

Excuse; Later Scripture overrules previous scriptures

Rebuttal: Here the Biblicists ignore that the superseding scripture in the Bible also confirms apostates are to be put to death;

"If we decide to go on sinning after we have learned the truth, there is no longer any sacrifice for sins. There is nothing but fear in waiting for the judgment and the terrible fire that will destroy all those who live against God. Anyone who refused to obey the law of Moses was found guilty from the proof given by two or three witnesses. He was put to death without mercy. So what do you think should be done to those who do not respect the Son of God, who look at the blood of the agreement that made them holy as no different from others' blood, who insult the Spirit of God's grace? Surely they should have a much worse punishment." (Hebrews 10:26-29)

Correction: Our Merciful Lord shows benevolence towards those who stray in error, giving the apostate more than one chance to repent. The Quran does not discard human lives ruthlessly as the Bible appears to:

"Those who believe, then reject faith, then believe (again) and (again) reject faith, and go on increasing in unbelief,- Allah will not forgive them nor guide them nor guide them on the way." (Quran 4:137)

Furthermore, in the Holy Quran, the death given to apostates is a spiritual one, where the rejecters of faith lose guidance:

"That is because they believed, then they rejected Faith: So a seal was set on their hearts: therefore they understand not." (Quran 63:3)

Unlike the Bible, the Quran teaches not to physically harm those who do not physically harm us:

"Let there be no compulsion in religion: Truth stands out clear from Error: whoever rejects evil and believes in Allah hath grasped the most trustworthy hand-hold that never breaks. And Allah heareth and knoweth all things." (Quran 2:256)

58. Blind Faith

Errancy; The Bible claims that people who are seeing impaired are desecrated, thus disqualified to be priests;

"The Lord said to Moses, "Say to Aaron, None of your descendants throughout their generations who has a blemish may approach to offer the bread of his God. For no one who has a blemish shall draw near, -a man blind or a defect in his sight- no man of the descendants of Aaron the priest who has a blemish shall come near to offer the Lord's offerings by fire; since he has a blemish, he shall not come near to offer the bread of his God. he shall not come near the veil or approach the altar, because he has a blemish, that he may not profane my sanctuaries; for I am the Lord who sanctify them." (Leviticus 21:16-23)

Excuse; None available.

Correction: (Continued from 58-64)

59. Lame?

Errancy; The Bible claims that people who are lame are defiled, thus disqualified to be priests;

"the Lord said to Moses, "Say to Aaron, None of your descendants throughout their generations who has a blemish may approach to offer the bread of his God. For no one who has a blemish shall draw near,-a man lame-, no man of the descendants of Aaron the priest who has a blemish shall come near to offer the Lord's offerings by fire; since he has a blemish, he shall not come near to offer the bread of his God. he shall not come near the veil or approach the altar, because he has a blemish, that he may not profane my sanctuaries; for I am the Lord who sanctify them." (Leviticus 21:16-23)

Excuse; None available.

Correction: (Continued from 58-64)

60. Facial appearance?

Errancy; The Bible claims that people who are facially disfigured, are debauched, thus disqualified to be priests;

"the Lord said to Moses, "Say to Aaron, None of your descendants throughout their generations who has a blemish may approach to offer the bread of his God. For no one who has a blemish shall draw near,-one who has a mutilated face-, no man of the descendants of Aaron the priest who has a blemish shall come near to offer the Lord's offerings by fire; since he has a blemish, he shall not come near to offer the bread of his God. he shall not come near the veil or approach the altar, because he has a blemish, that he may not profane my sanctuaries; for I am the Lord who sanctify them." (Leviticus 21:16-23)

Excuse; None available.

Correction: (Continued from 58-64)

61. Injured Foot?

Errancy; The Bible claims that people with an injured foot are debased, thus disqualified to be priests;

"the Lord said to Moses, "Say to Aaron, None of your descendants throughout their generations who has a blemish may approach to offer the bread of his God. For no one who has a blemish shall draw near,-a man who has an injured foot-, no man of the descendants of Aaron the priest who has a blemish shall come near to offer the Lord's offerings by fire; since he has a blemish, he shall not come near to offer the bread of his God. he shall not come near the veil or approach the altar, because he has a blemish, that he may not profane my sanctuaries; for I am the Lord who sanctify them." (Leviticus 21:16-23)

Excuse; None available.

Correction: (Continued from 58-64)

62. Injured Hand?

Errancy; The Bible claims that people with an injured hand are degraded, thus disqualified to be priests;

"the Lord said to Moses, "Say to Aaron, None of your descendants throughout their generations who has a blemish may approach to offer the bread of his God. For no one who has a blemish shall draw near,-injured hand-, no man of the descendants of Aaron the priest who has a blemish shall come near to offer the Lord's offerings by fire; since he has a blemish, he shall not come near to offer the bread of his God. he shall not come near the veil or approach the altar, because he has a blemish, that he may not profane my sanctuaries; for I am the Lord who sanctify them." (Leviticus 21:16-23)

Excuse; None available.

Correction: (Continued from 58-64)

63. Hunchback?

Errancy; The Bible claims that people with a hunchback are indecent, thus disqualified to be priests;

"the Lord said to Moses, "Say to Aaron, None of your descendants throughout their generations who has a blemish may approach to offer the bread of his God. For no one who has a blemish shall draw near,-a hunchback-, no man of the descendants of Aaron the priest who has a blemish shall come near to offer the Lord's offerings by fire; since he has a blemish, he shall not come near to offer the bread of his God. he shall not come near the veil or approach the altar, because he has a blemish, that he may not profane my sanctuaries; for I am the Lord who sanctify them." (Leviticus 21:16-23)

Excuse; None available.

Correction: (Continued from 58-64)

64. Restricted Growth?

Errancy; The Bible claims that people with restricted growth are indecent, thus disqualified to be priests;

"the Lord said to Moses, "Say to Aaron, None of your descendants throughout their generations who has a blemish may approach to offer the bread of his God. For no one who has a blemish shall draw near,-a man with restricted growth-, no man of the descendants of Aaron the priest who has a blemish shall come near to offer the Lord's offerings by fire; since he has a blemish, he shall not come near to offer the bread of his God. he shall not come near the veil or approach the altar, because he has a blemish, that he may not profane my sanctuaries; for I am the Lord who sanctify them." (Leviticus 21:16-23)

Excuse; None available.

Correction: The Quran corrects the Bible in that it does not differentiate between a human's physical form in relation to their benevolence.

Furthermore, if certain rituals cannot be fulfilled because of a person's physical limitations, the Holy Quran exempts the individual from any guilt and these people are equally promised Heaven just as other believers:

"No blame is there on the blind, nor is there blame on the lame, nor for the sick (if they do not go forth): But he that obeys Allah and his Messenger, - (Allah) will admit him to Gardens beneath which rivers flow; and he who turns back, (Allah) will punish him with a grievous Penalty. (Quran 48:17)

65. First Born?

Errancy; The Bible taught people to sacrifice their first-born sons;

"Thou shalt not delay to offer the first of thy ripe fruits, and of thy liquors: the firstborn of thy sons shalt thou give unto me." (Exodus 22:29)

Although the Bible records that this law was never followed, and instead the tribe of Levi was sacrificed instead (Numbers 3:12), it remains a horrid suggestion in the Bible.

Excuse; None available.

Correction: The Quran teaches that only fake gods made such an evil evocation. God is the Most Powerful and never needs to sacrifice a people for another but instead can do what He pleases without condemning innocent ones as a sacrifice:

"And thus their associates have made fair seeming to most of the polytheists the killing of their children that they may cause them to perish and obscure for them their religion; and if Allah had pleased, they would not have done it, therefore leave them and that which they forge." (Quran 6:137)

"Losers indeed are those who killed their children foolishly, due to their lack of knowledge, and prohibited what Allah has provided for them, and followed innovations attributed to Allah. They have gone astray; they are not guided." (Quran 6:140)

66. Polygamy?

Errancy; There is serious confusion in the Bible regarding polygamy. Polygamy was commonly practiced among Christian's centuries after Jesus. Polygamy was not outlawed until the 19th century and is still practiced by some Christian sects today.

The problem from the Bible is that the legality of Polygamy is unclear;

Polygamy approved (2 Samuel 12:8) *Vs* Polygamy not approved (Deuteronomy 17:17)

Polygamist Prophets in the Bible; [Abraham (Genesis 16:3)], [Jacob (Genesis 16)], [David (Genesis 29:30)], [Solomon (1 Kings 11:1-8)].

Excuse; Various Biblicists have different positions on this topic regarding their cultural inclination, till this day, there are still pro-polygamy Christians.

Rebuttal: Due to the Everlasting Covenant being made with Abraham, a polygamist, along with other blessed Prophets; it is impossible to classify polygamy as forbidden, for the most righteous men on earth partook in it.

Correction: The Holy Quran, unlike the Bible, gives clear rules regarding polygamy:

"If ye fear that ye shall not be able to deal justly with the orphans, Marry women of your choice, Two or three or four; but if ye fear that ye shall not be able to deal justly (with them), then only one, or (a captive) that your right hands possess, that will be more suitable, to prevent you from doing injustice." (Quran 4:3)

Unlike the various number of wives of different Prophets within the Bible (1 Kings 11:3), the Holy Quran limits the number of wives to four (with conditions), stating that if you can not treat the four wives equally, then only marry one for that is most just.

67. Swear an Oath?

Errancy; Making an oath approved (Deuteronomy 6:13, Numbers 30:2, Hebrews 6:13) *Vs* Making an oath not approved (Matthew 5:34, James 5:12)

Excuse; 1st) Taking an oath was permitted before Jesus, and abolished by Jesus. 2nd) There are different types of oaths and Jesus meant the frivolous ones are forbidden.

Rebuttal: 1st) Jesus did not abolish taking oaths because he himself [teaching by example], took an oath (Matthew 26:63-64). 2nd) Jesus and his brother James did not say 'some oaths' or 'certain oaths', both men clearly said "All oaths"

"But I say unto you, Swear not at all; neither by heaven; for it is God's throne" (Matthew 5:34)

And

"But above all things, my brethren, swear not, neither by heaven, neither by the earth, and neither by any other oath: but let your yea be yea; and your nay, nay; lest ye fall into condemnation." (James 5:12)

Correction: Making an oath is not a sin, unless one makes an oath while making the intention to break it. The Quran clears up the disorder created by the Bible writers:

"Allah will not take you to task for that which is unintentional in your oaths, but He will call you to account for your deliberate oaths: for expiation, feed ten indigent persons, on a scale of the average for the food of your families; or clothe them; or give a slave his freedom. If that is beyond your means, fast for three days. That is the expiation for the oaths ye have sworn. But keep to your oaths. Thus doth Allah make clear to you His signs, that ye may be grateful." (Quran 5:89)

68. Pleasant Words?

Errancy; Shall we call people names?

"Whoever says, 'You fool!' shall be liable to the hell of fire." (Matthew 5:22) *Vs* "[Jesus speaking] "Ye fools and blind." (Matthew 23:17)

Excuse; That is what it says but that is not what it means. The word 'fool' has different meanings in these different passages.

Rebuttal: (See Reply letter [E] in Rebuttal Chart) The word "fool" has no dual meaning. Whether the phrase is said angrily or softly, (which Jesus did both), the word still has the same meaning.

Correction: The Holy Quran clearly and consistently teaches us not to slander others:

"O ye who believe! Let not some men among you laugh at others: It may be that the (latter) are better than the (former): Nor let some women laugh at others: It may be that the (latter are better than the (former): Nor defame nor be sarcastic to each other, nor call each other by (offensive) nicknames: Ill-seeming is a name connoting wickedness, (to be used of one) after he has believed: And those who do not desist are (indeed) doing wrong." (Quran 49:11)

69. Enslaving Children?

Errancy; The Bible allows the selling of your own children to be slaves and provides legislation for such a transaction;

"And if a man sell his daughter to be a slave, she shall not go out as the men slaves do. If she pleases not her master, who hath betrothed her to himself, then shall he let her be redeemed: to sell her unto a strange nation he shall have no power, seeing he hath dealt deceitfully with her." (Exodus 21:7-8)

Excuse; None available.

Correction: The Holy Quran forbids humans enslaving other humans:

"It is not (possible) for any human being unto whom Allah had given the Scripture and wisdom and the prophethood that he should afterwards have said unto mankind: Be slaves of me instead of Allah; but (what he said was): Be ye faithful servants of the Lord by virtue of your constant teaching of the Scripture and of your constant study thereof." (Quran 3:79)

Second, the Holy Quran teaches to protect your children and not to forsake them for money:

"Slay not your children, for fear of poverty, We shall provide for them and for you. Surely the slaying of them is great sin." (Quran 17:31)

70. Laughing Legal?

Errancy; Laughter approved (Proverbs 17:22) *Vs* Laughter disapproved (Ecclesiastes 7:3-4)

Excuse; There is a time to laugh and there is a time to cry (Ecclesiastes 3:1-4)

Rebuttal: This statement is correct, yet the excuse is wrong. Both passages do not say "some laughter" or "laughter at certain times'. Instead, the context is clear; laughter will lead to sorrow, and not the other way around;

"Even in laughter the heart is sad, and the end of joy is grief." (Proverbs 14:13)

It is summed up that the Bible prefers sad people here;

"Come near to God, and he will come near to you. Wash your hands, you sinners! Purify your hearts, you hypocrites! Be sorrowful, cry, and weep; change your laughter into crying, your joy into gloom! Humble yourselves before the Lord, and he will lift you up." (James 4:8-10)

Correction: While God prefers the unhappy in the Bible, God in the Quran clarifies that laughter and sadness is all a part of the blessings that God provides to humans:

"That it is He (Allah) Who granteth Laughter and Tears" (Quran 53:43)

71. Talking to Others?

Errancy; Do not say anything to a non-believer (2 John 1:10 – 11) *Vs* Always answer a non-believer (1 Peter 3:15)

Excuse; These two passages are speaking of two different groups of people.

Rebuttal: The only difference is in the authors of the passages who both clearly express everyone and do not limit the speaking laws to an elite group.

Correction: In the matter of theological discussions, we are not asked to ostracize ourselves as in the Bible. Instead, just the opposite, we are told to encounter non-believers:

"Invite (all) to the Way of thy Lord with wisdom and beautiful preaching; and argue with them in ways that are best and most gracious: for thy Lord knoweth best, who have strayed from His Path, and who receive guidance." (Quran 16:125)

72. Dealing with Missionaries

Errancy; The Bible teaches that missionaries from religions other than yours, are to be put to death;

"But put to death any interpreters of dreams or prophets that tell you to rebel against the Lord, who rescued you from Egypt, where you were slaves. Such people are evil and are trying to lead you away from the life that the Lord has commanded you to live. They must be put to death, in order to rid yourselves of this evil." (Deuteronomy 13:5)

Excuse; None available.

Correction: God revealed to us in the Holy Quran to tolerate and even protect people of other faiths. If missionaries try to convert us to another religion, we are to politely respond;

"I worship not that which ye worship, Nor do you serve Him Whom I serve: Nor am I going to serve that which you serve, Nor are you going to serve Him Whom I serve: You shall have your religion and I shall have my religion." (Quran 109:2-6)

73. Give it All Away?

Errancy; The Bible teaches people to be an overly philanthropic spender;

"Give to every man that asketh of thee; and of him that taketh away thy goods ask them not again." (Luke 6:30)

Excuse; Jesus never said to give it –all- away;

Rebuttal: Actually, Jesus did say, "give it –all- away"; when a righteous person who kept all the commandments (Luke 18:21) asked Jesus how to attain eternal life, Jesus replied that the –one single thing he lacked- was;

"Yet lackest thou one thing: sell –all- that thou hast, and -distribute unto the poor, and thou shalt have treasure in heaven" (Luke 18:22)

Furthermore, regarding storing treasures on earth, Jesus says;

"And again I say unto you, It is easier for a camel to go through the eye of a needle, than for a rich man to enter into the kingdom of God." (Matthew 19:24)

Peter confirms that the disciples gave away –all- they had;

"Then answered Peter and said unto him, Behold, we have forsaken –all-, and followed thee; what shall we have therefore?" (Matthew 19:27)

And Jesus again reaffirms that for giving away all they had, they will be rewarded in Heaven;

"Jesus said to them, "You can be sure that when the Son of Man sits on his glorious throne in the New Age, then you twelve followers of mine will also sit on thrones, to rule the twelve tribes of Israel." (Matthew 19:28)

Therefore, Jesus teaches the righteous to give it –all- away.

Correction: The Quran removes the error of this bankrupting law in the Bible by stating:

"And render to the kindred their due rights, as (also) to those in want, and to the wayfarer: But squander not (your wealth) in the manner of a spendthrift." (Quran 17: 26)

"And they who when they spend, are neither extravagant nor parsimonious, but hold a just (balance) between those (extremes)" (Quran 25:67)

74. Sermon Contempt

Errancy; In the Bible, one who argues with a priest is to be put to death;

"The man who shows contempt for the judge or for the priest who stands ministering there to the Lord your God must be put to death." (Deuteronomy 17:12)

Excuse; None available.

Correction: Unlike the Bible, the Quran encourages freedom of speech. The Quran shows that women can even argue with the Prophet:

"Allah hath heard the saying of her that disputeth with thee (Muhammad) concerning her husband, and complaineth unto Allah. and Allah (always) hears the arguments between both sides among you: for Allah hears and sees (all things)." (Quran 58:1)

75. Obey Parents in all?

Errancy; Obey your parents in all things (Colossians 3:20) *Vs* Do not obey your parents in all things (Matthew 10:37)

Excuse; You must understand the context of the verse. (Colossians 3:20) intends to say "all things that please the Lord"

Rebuttal: What is intended and what is said is in they eyes of the interpreter. We know that structurally, the passage states that no matter what the parents tell you to do, God will be pleased because you obeyed them.

Correction: The Holy Quran clearly sets the boundaries in obeying our parents. Kindness in all matters is ordained for us towards our parents, yet we are not to obey our parents if obeying them will conflict with obeying God, The Resolver, for God's orders are always to be obeyed above our parents' orders.

"And We have enjoined on man (to be good) to his parents: in travail upon travail did his mother bear him, and in years twain was his weaning: (hear the command), "Show gratitude to Me and to thy parents:

to Me is (thy final) Goal. But if they strive to make thee join in worship with Me things of which thou hast no knowledge, obey them not; yet bear them company in this life with justice (and consideration), and follow the way of those who turn to me (in love): in the end the return of you all is to Me, and I will tell you the truth (and meaning) of all that ye did." (Quran 31:14-15)

76. Israel Conditional?

Errancy; Israel is given to Jews without condition (Genesis 12:1-3) *Vs* with conditions. (Deuteronomy 31:16–17)

Excuse; The eternal promise is to a far off future descendants of Abraham's appearing at the time of Christ's return.

Rebuttal: The context shows that the promise was never conditional to begin with. It was always conditional just as Adam and Eve's stay in the Garden of Eden was conditional. Why would God allow Jews to have an unconditional stay and not grant the same blessings of our ancestral parents? Second, we know the conditions were speaking of present and not future tense because of the punishments that occurred upon the Jews;

"And Samuel said to him, "The Lord has torn the kingdom of Israel from you this day, and has given it to a neighbor of yours, who is better than you." (1 Samuel 15:28)

Correction: The Quran teaches that God is a Just and Fair God who gives us accountability, hence does not unconditionally allow people to sin as the Bible suggests, for even the covenant with Abraham was conditional because God does not give blessings to evil doers:

"And remember when his Lord tried Abraham with words, and he fulfilled them, He said: Verily, I will set thee as a leader for the nations. Said he: And of my seed also? Allah said: My covenant touches not the evildoers." (Quran 2:124)

"But if ye turn your backs, then I have conveyed to you that wherewith I was sent to you; and my Lord will replace you with another people. Ye cannot harm (frustrate) Him at all; verily, my Lord is Guardian over all things!" (Quran 11:57)

77. Incest Allowed?

Errancy; Incest forbidden (Leviticus 18:6; 20:17) *Vs* Incest allowed (Genesis 19:30-38).

Excuse; Lot's long stay with the people of Sodom tainted his judgment and the narrative does not approve of incest.

Rebuttal: First, environmental influences is not an excuse for the Bible's account of Prophet Lot. Second, the Bible inadvertently endorses incest because the trio were not tormented, instead they begat great nations; Moab and Ammon.

Correction: First, the Quran does not confirm this degrading account of Prophet Lot. Second, the Quran clearly denounces incest without conflict;

"Prohibited to you (For marriage) are:- Your mothers, daughters, sisters; father's sisters, Mother's sisters; brother's daughters, sister's daughters; foster-mothers (Who gave you suck), foster-sisters; your wives' mothers; your step-daughters under your guardianship, born of your wives to whom ye have gone in,- no prohibition if ye have not gone in;- (Those who have been) wives of your sons proceeding from your loins; and two sisters in wedlock at one and the same time, except for what is past; for Allah is Oft-forgiving, Most Merciful" (Quran 4:23)

78. <u>Divorced man's rights</u>

Errancy; One of the problems in the Bible is the condemnation of divorced men. Once a man has been with a woman (in a marital relationship) the man (now divorced) naturally desires to remarry, yet the Bible states that the marriage to a divorced man is punishable by death;

"He said to them, "A man who divorces his wife and marries another woman commits adultery against his wife." (Mark 10:11)

Jesus equated divorce with adultery and adultery was punishable by stoning to death.

Excuse; None available.

Correction: The Holy Quran corrects this confinement in the Bible by stating that it is permissible for divorced men to remarry:

"A divorce is only permissible twice: after that, the parties should either hold Together on equitable terms, or separate with kindness. It is not lawful for you, (Men), to take back any of your gifts (from your wives), except when both parties fear that they would be unable to keep the limits ordained by Allah. If ye (judges) do indeed fear that they would be unable to keep the limits ordained by Allah, there is no blame on either of them if she gives something for her freedom. These are the limits ordained by Allah; so do not transgress them if any do transgress the limits ordained by Allah, such persons wrong (Themselves as well as others)."

"So if a husband divorces his wife (the third time), He cannot, after that, re-marry her until after she has married another husband and He has divorced her. In that case, there is no blame on either of them if they re-unite, provided they feel that they can keep the limits ordained by Allah. Such are the limits ordained by Allah, which He makes plain to those who understand." (Quran 2:229-30)

Thus, it is not sinful to be divorced and remarry for either the man or the woman.

(V.) History

79. Adam's Sentence

Errancy; Adam was sentenced to die the day he ate from the forbidden tree. (Genesis 2:17) *Vs* Adam lived 930 years. (Genesis 5:5)

Excuse; 1st) Adam died a spiritual death. 2nd) Adam began to slowly die physically.

Rebuttal: 1st) Adam neither died a spiritual or physical death after eating from the tree because;

Adam still spoke with God after eating from the tree, proving spiritual life (Genesis 3:9-22)

Adam and Eve had children, proving spiritual life (Genesis 4:1)

The descendants of Adam were blessed proving spiritual life (Genesis 6:18)

Adam is called the son of God, proving spiritual life (Luke 3:38)
Jesus is called the second Adam, proving spiritual life (1 Corinthians 15:45)

2nd) Living for almost a millennium shows that Adam had plenty of physical life. Furthermore, God did not say "you will start to die", instead the declaration was "You must not eat the fruit of that tree; if you do, you will die the same day." (Genesis 2:17). In conclusion, the claim that eventual death came is invalid because God did not say you will die a millennium later, yet instead God said Adam would die that same day. Lastly, in Biblical context, we know when God says, "you will die," God means instant physical death. For example;

A) "Keep the Sabbath, and honor the place where I am worshiped. I am the Lord." (Leviticus 19:30)
B) "Once, while the Israelites were still in the wilderness, a man was found gathering firewood on the Sabbath." (Numbers 15:32)
C) "Then the Lord said to Moses, "The man must be put to death; the whole community is to stone him to death outside the camp." (Numbers 15:35)

In conclusion, in the first half of the Bible, disobeying God bought immediate physical death, not a millennium long fruitful life.

Correction: The Holy Quran explains that Adam was caused to fall from one status to another; in fact, the Quran consistently confirms that Adam was meant to live on earth for a set time:

"But Satan caused them to slip there from and expelled them from the (happy) state in which they were; and We said: Fall down, one of you a foe unto the other! There shall be for you on earth a habitation and provision for a time." (Quran 2:36)

80. Adam's Reconciliation

Errancy; According to the Bible, Adam was not forgiven throughout his entire lifetime for eating from the forbidden tree. Adam is portrayed in the Bible as a non-repenting sinner throughout his entire life. Because Adam disobeyed God, Adam and all men and women after Adam were cursed and ejected from paradise. We see that even after Jesus came and left the world, Paul still speaks of the accursed Adam;

"Wherefore, as by one man [Adam] sin entered into the world, and death by sin; and so death passed upon all men, for that all have sinned" (Romans 5:12, 14, 1 Corinthians 15:21-22)

Furthermore, the Bible has no record of Adam repenting, ludicrously though; the Bible says God repented for making Adam (Genesis 6:6)

Thus, the Bible backwardly claims that it was God who repented rather than the one who disobeyed Him, Adam.

Excuse; None available.

Correction: The Holy Quran corrects the regressive passages that are found within the Bible, clarifying that it was Adam, not God who repented. Hence, God in the Quran provides the missing reconciliation that granted Adam and his descendants to have an ongoing communication with God:

"Then Adam received from his Lord words (of revelation), and He relented toward him. Lo! He is the Relenting the Merciful. We said: Go down, all of you, from hence; but verily there cometh unto you from Me a guidance; and whoso followeth My guidance, there shall no fear come upon them neither shall they grieve." (Quran 2:37-38)

81. Curse of Babylon?

Errancy; According to the Bible, the entire world used to speak one language. These ancient people were trying to build a tower to see God.

As a punishment for their audacity, God placed a curse on them, making them all speak a different language. This tower is now called the "Tower of Babylon". (Genesis 11:9) and hence the word "Babble".

According to the Bible, we are still afflicted with this curse because Bible followers' world wide still worship God in various languages and recite Bibles in different languages. Bible followers still babble among themselves and do not yet worship in unison;

"For then will I turn to the people a pure language that they may all call upon the name of the Lord, to serve him with one consent." (Zephaniah 3:9)

In the Strong's Bible Dictionary, the word "language (saphah)" in this verse can also mean [side, edge, border]

Therefore, (Zephaniah 3:9) has the dual meaning "I will –turn- people to –one- direction, which Bible followers do not do, each church world wide faces disorganized directions.

Excuse; None available.

Correction: The Holy Quran was revealed and preserved in its original language as a Mercy from God. When humans return to pure monotheism and obedience to God, then the curse of Babylon is removed.

The Quran removes the curse of Babylon by inspiring the believers world wide to recite and pray using God's words in the melodious Arabic language. This is astonishing since only 27% of the Muslims are Arabs and there are almost 1.5 Billion Muslims worldwide, all united with one language, praying in unison as foretold in the Bible and fulfilled through the Quran.

In conclusion, through the power, magnificence, and truth of the Quran, the curse described in the Bible is being erased. The Bible does not cure the curse of Babylon because the Bible is accepted in all languages, spreading the curse of Babylon and diluting the original message of God, while the Quran remains in its original, authentic, curse free language.

In ten different verses in the Holy Quran, it is stated that the Quran is sent in Arabic, hence preserved, memorized, and recited in Arabic to protect the scripture from mistranslations.

"A Lecture in Arabic, containing no crookedness that haply they may ward off (evil)." (Quran 39:28)

Besides the pure language, the Quran also fulfils the dual of (Zephaniah 3:9) because we witness that Muslims all face the East to pray. Thus, we as Muslims turn to one direction and worship in one language, removing the curse of Babylon.

82. Noah's Flood (Global or Local)

Errancy; The Bible claims Noah's Flood drowned the entire world;

"And all flesh died that moved on the earth: birds and cattle and beasts and every creeping thing that creeps on the earth, and every man. All in whose nostrils was the breath of the spirit of life, all that was on the dry land, died. So He destroyed all living things which were on the face of the ground: both man and cattle, creeping thing and bird of the air. They were destroyed from the earth. Only Noah and those who were with him in the ark remained alive." (Genesis 7:21-23)

Besides this being an unfair collective punishment towards the human race, the Bible also conflicts with history.

At the same time of the flood, there were prosperous civilizations such as the Egyptian's Eleventh Dynasty and Babylonia's Third Dynasty at Ur.

Excuse; The story of a great flood is told by the Greeks, the Hindus, the Chinese, the Mexicans, the Algonquins, and the Hawaiians. Also, one list of Sumerian kings also treat the Flood as a real event.

Rebuttal: If there was a Flood and Noah's kin were the only survivors, then there was not anyone left in all those other locations to tell the story. We have to admit that these worldwide stories do not prove that the Flood occurred in all these places because then life would have ceased for over year, leaving no other culture to tell the story, according to the Bible.

Correction: In contrast, the Quran mentions intended flooding incidents inflicted on specific transgressing groups. This is viewed in (Quran 25: 35-40):

"We gave Moses the Scripture and appointed his brother Aaron with him as vizier. We said: Go to the people who have denied Our signs. We destroyed them completely. When the people of Noah denied the Messengers, We drowned them and We made of them a sign for humankind. (We destroyed the tribes) of Ad and Tamud, the companions of Rass and many generations between them. We warned each of them by examples and We annihilated them completely. And the (Unbelievers) must indeed have passed by the town on which was rained a fatal shower: did they not then see it (with their own eyes)? But they fear not the Resurrection."

(Quran 7:59 to 93) contains a reminder of the punishments brought upon Noah's people, the Ad, the Tamud, Lot (Sodom) and Madian respectively.

As a result, the Quran rescues the Bible regarding the narration of the Flood.

83. <u>One or Seven Pairs?</u>

Errancy; Noah takes one pair of animal onto the ark (Genesis 6:19) *Vs* Noah takes seven of each type of animal onto the ark (Genesis 7:2-3)

Excuse; (Genesis 7:2-3) is speaking of seven clean animals and (Genesis 6:19) is speaking of one pair of unclean animal. 2nd) The clean animals were meant to be sacrificed, while the unclean animals were meant to be kept alive, that is why there were more of the clean animals taken on board.

Rebuttal: 1st) (Genesis 6:19) says to take one pair of every type of animal, and does not differentiate between clean or unclean animals as the apologetics assume. 2nd) Noah was on board the ark for over a year (Genesis 8: 15–17) giving all the animals, whether clean or unclean, ample time to multiply, thus invalidating the need to take more of any particular type. Lastly, the seven of each clean animals were also intended to be kept alive because (Genesis 7:2) says; "seven each of every clean animal, a male and his female" which clarifies that they were intended to breed and stay alive.

Correction: Sensibly, seven pairs of species would have been excessive, especially since they spent seasons at sea, where new seeds surely sprung. The Quran corrects the discrepant amount of animals noted in the Bible by stating:

"(Thus it was) till, when Our commandment came to pass and the oven gushed forth water, We said: Load therein two of every kind, a pair (the male and female), and thy household, save him against whom the word hath gone forth already, and those who believe. And but a few were they who believed with him." (Quran 11:40)

84. First to Ascend?

Errancy; No one has ascended into heaven before Jesus (John 3:13) *Vs* Elijah ascended into heaven (2 Kings 2:11)

Excuse; That is what it says but that is not what it means. Jesus means that no one went to heaven and returned with a message before him.

Rebuttal: (See Reply letter [E] in Rebuttal Chart). This is an insertion by apologetics with no basis in context or meaning of the passage.

Besides this excuse being unfounded, it's also incorrect because Elijah is shown within the Bible to have ascended to Heaven and did indeed return with a message before Jesus;

"But I say to you that Elijah has come already, and they did not know him but did to him whatever they wished. Likewise the Son of Man is also about to suffer at their hands." (Matthew 17:12)

Correction: Unlike the conflicting Bible, the Noble Quran confirms that others before Jesus have ascended into Heaven;

"And (the Jinn who had listened to the Quran said): We had sought the heaven but had found it filled with strong warders and meteors." (Quran 72:8)

85. Joseph's Prophecy

Errancy; The Bible manifests an unfulfilled prophecy concerning Joseph's dream;

"Then he (Joseph) had another dream, and he told it to his Brothers. "Listen," he said, "I had another dream, and this time the sun and moon and eleven stars were bowing down to me." (Genesis 37:9)

Although the Bible mentions Prophet Joseph's dream, the Bible never shows that his dream was fulfilled. The reason why the Bible does not complete Joseph's dream is due to an irreconcilable sequence of events.

In the Bible, the mother of Prophet Joseph supposedly died when she bore Benjamin.

"And as she was having great difficulty in childbirth, the midwife said to her, "Don't be afraid, for you have another son." As she breathed her last—for she was dying—she named her son Ben-Oni. But his father named him Benjamin. So Rachel died and was buried on the way to Ephrath (that is, Bethlehem). (Genesis 35:17-19)

Rachel is the mother of Joseph and Benjamin; In the Bible, she died two Chapters before Joseph had his dream.

Excuse; None available.

Correction: The Quran mentions this dream at the beginning of the Chapter entitled (Joseph), and shows how it was implemented and thus, fulfilled:

"(Remember) when Yusuf (Joseph) said to his father: "O my father! Verily, I saw (in a dream) eleven stars and the sun and the moon, I saw them prostrating themselves to me." (Quran 12:4)

The Quran never says that his mother died, the proof for this is at the end of the story where Joseph raises both of his parents on his throne.

"And he raised his parents high on the throne (of dignity), and they fell down in prostration, (all) before him. He said: "O my father! this is the fulfillment of my vision of old! Allah hath made it come true! He was indeed good to me when He took me out of prison and brought you (all here) out of the desert, (even) after Satan had sown enmity between me and my brothers. Verily my Lord understandeth best the mysteries of all that He planneth to do, for verily He is full of knowledge and wisdom." (Quran 12:100)

In the Quran, the dream was realized when his father (The Sun) and his mother (the Moon) and his eleven brothers (stars) bowed down to him.

Bible writers make a mistake when they claim that Joseph's mother died before the adventures of Joseph happened. The Quran clears the divergences that have been injected within Bible.

86. The Sale of Joseph?

Errancy; There are two opposing statements pertaining to the buyer of Joseph in the Bible;

"Then there passed by Midianites merchantmen; and they drew and lifted up Joseph out of the pit, and sold Joseph to the Ishmaelites for twenty pieces of silver: and they brought Joseph into Egypt." (Genesis 37:28).

Midianites sold Joseph outside of Egypt to the Ishmaelites

"Meanwhile the Midianites had sold him in Egypt to Potiphar, an officer of Pharaoh, the captain of the guard." (Genesis 37:36)

Midianites sold Joseph inside Egypt to Potiphar

"Now Joseph had been taken down to Egypt; and Potiphar, an Egyptian officer of Pharaoh, the captain of the bodyguard, bought him from the Ishmaelites, who had taken him down there." (Genesis 39:1)

Potiphar purchased Joseph from the Ishmaelites, not the Midianites.

Excuse; Some Bible apologists attempt to amend this contrariety by claiming the "Midianites" and the "Ishmaelites" are the same people. This red herring attempt by Bible proponents argue; because the Ishmaelites were in Midian (Judges 8:22-24), Midianites and Ishmaelites are one in the same.

Rebuttal: Such Biblical advocates lack a degree of knowledge of the genealogy of Abraham, Hebrew terminology, and the travel custom of the ancient tribes.

First, the Ishmaelites are descendants of Ishmael, the son of Abraham through his wife Hagar, while the Midianites are the descendants of Midian, the son of Abraham through his wife Keturah. Ishmaelites and Midianites are clearly from two separate lineages.

Centuries of Bible followers have been trying to delegitimize Ishmael because he came from Hagar, yet when faced with a Bible difficulty, these Bible apologetics are quickly trying to reverse course and associate the Ishmaelites with an unarguably legitimate son, (Genesis 25:1-4) Midian. What is forgotten is that these two sons are not interchangeable.

Second, the *KJV Old Testament Hebrew Lexicon* states;

Midianite = "a member of the tribe of Midian."
Ishmaelite = "a descendant of Ishmael."

Once again, the two are not interchangeable.

Third, these ancient tribes had nomadic behavior, journeying from land to land, Abraham himself came from Ur (modern day Iraq), traveled to Haran (Genesis 11:31), then to Canaan (Genesis 12:4-5), then to Bethel (Genesis 12:8), then to Egypt (Genesis 12:10-20) and then to Gerar (Genesis 20:1). Using the apologist's defense, one can also allege Abraham was a Canaanite or an Egyptian. Who or what a person is, is not interchangeable.

Lastly, (Genesis 37:28) signifies that the Midianites are different from the Ishmaelites because the Bible does not say, "the Midianites sold Joseph to their 'brethren' or 'among themselves'", which are very common terms in the Bible, instead a different group is specified; the "Ishmaelites". Therefore, the Ishmaelites are from a different tribe. The Midianites and Ishmaelites may have been together for a time and may have even been related, but the scribes saw enough difference to document their different origins. Therefore, the unanswered questions still remain; who, when, and where? Was Joseph sold to the Ishmaelites before entrance to Egypt or directly to Potiphar while in Egypt and was the sale by the Midianites, in or out of Egypt?

Correction: The Quran clearly and consistently calls the buyer "An Egyptian";

"And the Egyptian who bought him, said to his wife: "Make his stay (among us) honorable: may be he will bring us much good, or we shall adopt him as a son." Thus did We establish Joseph in the land, that We might teach him the interpretation of stories (and events). And Allah hath full power and control over His affairs; but most among mankind know it not." (Quran 12:21)

Instead of confusing and inconsistent tribe swapping in or out of Egypt witnessed in the Bible, we thankfully have the Quran which corrects; the who, when, and where by clearly stating that Joseph was sold to an Egyptian.

Some Christian missionaries, who are unfamiliar with Arabic, ignorantly claim the Quran names the buyer as "Aziz". The word used in the Quran is "al-aziz", not "Aziz" as incorrectly understood by these polemicists. "al aziz" is a title meaning "chief" or "ruler", not a name as simplified in both the Pickthal and Shakir translations of the Quran;

"And women in the city said: The ruler's wife is asking of her slave-boy an ill-deed. Indeed he has smitten her to the heart with love. We behold her in plain aberration." (Quran 12:30)

"And women in the city said: The chiefs wife seeks her slave to yield himself (to her), surely he has affected her deeply with (his) love; most surely we see her in manifest error." (Quran 12:30)

In the *Yusuf Ali Translation with commentary*, which does use the word "al aziz" rather than "chief" or "ruler", the commentary explains the reason for the choice of words;

"I have not translated the title but left it as it is. Excellency or Highness would have specialized modern associations which I want to avoid" (*Yusuf Ali Translation with commentary*: pg. 1677)

In conclusion, the Quran accurately calls the buyer an Egyptian chief, thus settling the entire transaction with a gleaming verse, ordaining together the directionless verses in the Bible.

87. Abraham's Father?

Errancy; The Bible contains conflicts surrounding Abraham's Father

In (Genesis 11:26), Abraham's Father is called "Terah", yet in (Luke 3:34), Abraham's Father is called "Thara"

Also, in various Talmudic stories (Midr. Rabbah on Gen. par. 17), Abraham's father is called "Zarah", while Eusebius Pamphili (the ecclesiastical) gives his name as Athar.

Excuse; Translation error

Rebuttal: (See Reply letter [I] in Rebuttal Chart).

Correction: The Quran corrects all the skepticism surrounding the identity of Abraham's father by naming him "Azar" (Quran 6:74), similar to the Greek name Athar as used by Biblical scholars. The Quran stands firm on the identity of Abraham's father and does not present paradoxes pertaining to his name, age, and progeny, as does the Bible.

88. Abraham's Sacrifice?

Errancy; Who was the sacrificial son of Abraham? The Bible claims Isaac was the son to be sacrificed, yet logically and mathematically, the son was Ishmael.

The covenant was first made with Abraham and Ishmael;

"This [is] my covenant, which ye shall keep, between me and you and thy seed after thee; Every man child among you shall be circumcised." (Genesis 17:10)

"He that is born in thy house, and he that is bought with thy money, must needs be circumcised: and my covenant shall be in your flesh for an everlasting covenant." (Genesis 17:13)

The arithmetic of Abraham's age reveals that Ishmael was the son to be sacrificed;

"and Abram [is] a son of eighty and six years in Hagar's bearing Ishmael to Abram." (Genesis 16:16)

"Abraham was ninety-nine years old when he was circumcised in the flesh of his foreskin." (Genesis 17:24)

That makes Abraham's son Ishmael 13, how old is Isaac at this time?

"Abraham was a hundred years old when his son Isaac was born to him." (Genesis 21:5)

That means during the prepared sacrifice, Abraham's only "begotten" son is Ishmael and not Isaac as the Bible conflictingly says (Hebrews 11:17)

Therefore, we see that Isaac was not the only son, in fact, Isaac was not even born yet, and Abraham's only begotten son was Ishmael.

Furthermore, we know that Ishmael has and will be a legitimate son, despite what some Bible commentator's claim;

(Genesis 16:3) "And Sarai Abram's wife took Hagar her maid the Egyptian, after Abram had dwelt ten years in the land of Canaan, and gave her to her husband Abram to be his wife."

(Genesis 25:9) "Then his sons Isaac and Ishmael buried him (Abraham) in the cave of Machpelah, in the field of Ephron the son of Zohar the Hittite, facing Mamre,"

(Genesis 25:12) "Now these are the records of the generations of Ishmael, Abraham's son, whom Hagar the Egyptian, Sarah's maid, bore to Abraham;"

Excuse; Due to the mother of Ishmael being a bonds woman, Ishmael was not a legitimate son.

Rebuttal: This excuse is discredited by the passage;

"And Sarah Abram's wife took Hagar her maid the Egyptian, after Abram had dwelt ten years in the land of Canaan, and gave her to her husband Abram to be his wife." (Genesis 16:3)

Therefore, unless the Biblicists are claiming Abraham committed adultery; Hagar was a legitimate wife of Abraham and consequently, Ishmael was a legitimate son of Abraham. Further proof is;

"Then his sons Isaac and Ishmael buried him (Abraham) in the cave of Machpelah, in the field of Ephron the son of Zohar the Hittite, facing Mamre," (Genesis 25:9)

Here, the Bible directly calls Ishmael a son (not stepson or half son) of Abraham, standing equally in front of the grave with Isaac. Although, at one point Abraham and Hagar were separated, that does not invalidate the child Hagar had with Abraham. For example, if two parents get a divorce, the father and son lineage is not broken, even if the father may not have custody, the son is still the child of the father.

Correction: These mistaken identities and miscalculations in the Bible are amended by the Quran listing the correct chronological order, Ishmael being born, the sacrifice to be taken place, and then Isaac being born (continued from 88 to 89)

89. <u>One or Two Sons?</u>

Errancy; How many children did Abraham have?

One son "And He said, "Take now your son, your only son, whom you love, Isaac, and go to the land of Moriah; and offer him there as a burnt offering on one of the mountains of which I will tell you." (Genesis 22:2)

Vs

Two sons "For it is written that Abraham had two sons, one by the bondwoman and one by the free woman." (Galatians 4:22)

Excuse; Due to the mother of Ishmael being a bonds woman, Ishmael was not a legitimate son.

Rebuttal: This excuse is discredited by the passage;

"And Sarah Abram's wife took Hagar her maid the Egyptian, after Abram had dwelt ten years in the land of Canaan, and gave her to her husband Abram to be his wife." (Genesis 16:3)

Therefore, unless the Biblicists are claiming Abraham committed adultery; Hagar was a legitimate wife of Abraham and consequently, Ishmael was a legitimate son of Abraham.
Further proof is;

"Then his sons Isaac and Ishmael buried him (Abraham) in the cave of Machpelah, in the field of Ephron the son of Zohar the Hittite, facing Mamre," (Genesis 25:9)

Here, the Bible directly calls Ishmael a son (not stepson or half son) of Abraham, standing equally in front of the grave with Isaac. Although, at one point Abraham and Hagar were separated, that does not invalidate the child Hagar had with Abraham. For example, if two parents get a divorce, the father and son lineage is not broken, even if the father may not have custody, the son is still the child of the father.

Correction: These mistaken identities and miscalculations in the Bible are amended by the Quran listing the correct chronological order;

(Quran 37:99) He said: "I will go to my Lord! He will surely guide me!
(Quran 37:100) "O my Lord! Grant me a righteous (son)!"

(Quran 37:101) So We gave him the good news of a forbearing son.
(Quran 37:102) Then, when (the son) reached (the age of) (serious) work with him, he said: "O my son! I have seen in a vision that I offer thee in sacrifice: now see what is thy view!" (The son) said: "O my father! Do as thou art commanded: thou will find me, if Allah so wills, one of the steadfast!"
(Quran 37:103) So when they had both submitted (to Allah), and he had laid him prostrate on his forehead (for sacrifice),
(Quran 37:104) We called out to him "O Abraham! ..
(Quran 37:105) "Thou hast already fulfilled the vision!" - thus indeed do We reward those who do right.
(Quran 37:106) For this was a clear trial-
(Quran 37:107) And We ransomed him with a momentous sacrifice:
(Quran 37:108) And We left for him among generations (to come) in later times:
(Quran 37:109) "Peace and salutation to Abraham!"
(Quran 37:110) Thus indeed do We reward those who do right.
(Quran 37:111) For he was one of Our believing Servants.
(Quran 37:112) And We gave him the good news of Isaac - a prophet, - one of the Righteous.

Thus, the Quran shows Abraham indeed bore two sons, Ishmael and Isaac.

90. David *Vs* Goliath?

Errancy; Who killed Goliath? The Bible appears to not agree with itself regarding the treasured defeat of the "greatest fighter" Goliath. This seems to be an ongoing pattern of name changing throughout the Bible, giving credit where credit is not due.

Two different people claim victory against Goliath in the Bible;

David did - "Thus David prevailed over the Philistine with a sling and a stone, and he struck the Philistine and killed him; but there was no sword in David's hand." (1 Samuel 17:50)

Elhanan did - "And there was war with the Philistines again at Gob, and Elhanan the son of Jaare-oregim the Bethlehemite killed Goliath the Gittite, the shaft of whose spear was like a weaver's beam." (2 Samuel 21:19)

Excuse; Copyist error.

Rebuttal: (See Reply letter [F] in Rebuttal Chart)

Correction: The true and only champion against Goliath is David, which is confirmed without a doubt in the Holy Quran;

"By Allah's will they routed them; and David slew Goliath; and Allah gave him the kingdom and wisdom, and taught him of that which He willeth. And if Allah had not repelled some men by others the earth would have been corrupted. But Allah is a Lord of Kindness to (His) creatures." (Quran 2:251)

In conclusion, another name has been corrected in the Bible by the Holy Quran.

91. Feared Pharaoh?

Errancy; Moses feared Pharaoh (Exodus 2:14-15) *Vs* Moses did not fear Pharaoh (Hebrews 11:27)

Excuse; None available.

Correction: Moses was a righteous messenger sent by God to face the evil magic of Pharaoh. After being inspired by God, Moses did not fear Pharaoh or he would have never boldly gone to him. Instead of being a fearful cowardice as wrongfully revealed in the Bible, Moses' true nature of being a source of comfort and security for the people of Israel is displayed. The Quran clarifies the scenario:

"So I fled from you (all) when I feared you; but my Lord has (since) invested me with judgment (and wisdom) and appointed me as one of the messengers." (Quran 26:21)

The Holy Quran consistently fills in the missing puzzle piece to correct the Bible.

"And We inspired Moses (saying): Throw thy staff! And lo! it swallowed up their lying show." (Quran 7:117)

"And when the terror fell on them they cried: O Moses! Pray for us unto thy Lord, because He hath a covenant with thee. If thou removest the terror from us we verily will trust thee and will let the Children of Israel go with thee. But when We did remove from them the terror for a term which they must reach, behold! they broke their Covenant" (Quran 7:134-135)

92. Why Lot's wife died

Errancy; Lot's wife died a horrible death with no valid explanation except that she turned around while the town was being destroyed.

According to the Bible, she was righteous and did not deserve to die because the angels of God themselves urged Lot to rescue her;

"With the coming of dawn, the angels urged Lot, saying, "Hurry! Take your wife and your two daughters who are here, or you will be swept away when the city is punished." (Genesis 19:15)

As they ran away from their town which was about to be destroyed by God, Lot's wife turned around (surely a natural reaction, having heard havoc and destruction behind her). When she turned around in the Bible, she was unjustly annihilated;

"But Lot's wife looked back and was turned into a pillar of salt" (Genesis 19:26)

Excuse; Lot's wife was destroyed because she disobeyed the angel who said;

"Run for your lives! Don't look back and don't stop in the valley. Run to the hills, so that you won't be killed." (Genesis 19:17)

Rebuttal: This is an invalid excuse because Lot did even worse. Lot not only stopped (a direct defiance to the angel's instructions), but also argued with them;

"But Lot answered, "No, please don't make us do that, sir. You have done me a great favor and saved my life. But the hills are too far away; the disaster will overtake me, and I will die before I get there. Do you see that little town? It is near enough. Let me go over there—you can see it is just a small place—and I will be safe." (Genesis 19:18-20)

After stopping to argue with the angel, Lot was not destroyed, thus invalidating that excuse. Furthermore, Lot appears suspiciously selfish when arguing with the angel, repeatedly saying, "so I can be safe", rather than including his wife who was not killed yet by stating; "so we can be safe".

Correction: What appears as unjustified and incompetence in the Bible (a Prophet and the angels of God could not rescue the wife), is actually comprehended in the Quran. The Quran explains why Prophet Lot's wife died;

"And We rescued him and his household, except his wife, who was of those who stayed behind." (Quran 7: 83)

"Allah citeth an example for those who disbelieve: the wife of Noah and the wife of Lot, who were under two of our righteous servants yet betrayed them so that they (the husbands availed them naught against Allah and it was said (unto them): Enter the Fire along with those who enter." (Quran 66:10)

The Holy Quran explains that the fact of the matter was Lot's wife stayed a transgressor who was destroyed among the other non-believers of Lot.

93. Israel Saved?

Errancy; All of Israel saved (Romans 11:26) *Vs* Israel not saved (Luke 12:9, John 1:11)

Excuse; Paul is speaking of the unconditional promise given to Israel;

"I am going to give you and your descendants all the land that you see, and it will be yours forever." (Genesis 13:15)

Rebuttal: This only expands the contradiction rather than contracts it. If Genesis says Israel will be saved forever, then again this contradicts the Bible which says that Israel will be cursed forever, because once saved (Genesis 13:15), then to reject salvation (Romans 5:9), results in damnation;

"For how can those who abandon their faith be brought back to repent again? They were once in God's light; they tasted heaven's gift and received their share of the Holy Spirit; they knew from experience that God's word is good, and they had felt the powers of the coming age. And then they abandoned their faith! It is impossible to bring them back to repent again, because they are again crucifying the Son of God and exposing him to public shame." (Hebrews 6:4-6)

This is also verified in Bible, which states that Israel can fall out of salvation;

"And Samuel said to him, "The Lord has torn the kingdom of Israel from you this day, and has given it to a neighbor of yours, who is better than you." (1 Samuel 15:28)

In conclusion, the nation of Israel, like everyone else on earth, is judged according to its faith and actions and is blessed or cursed based on the laws and conditions stated by God. Jesus was correct in saying those who reject his prophethood will be rejected in the Afterlife, while Paul was wrong to claim an unconditional salvation towards the nation of Israel, which both Jesus and the Bible rebuff.

Correction: The Holy Quran explains that each individual is judged for his or her own actions:

"Surely Allah does not do injustice to the weight of an atom, and if it is a good deed He multiplies it and gives from Himself a great reward." (Quran 4:40)

The Holy Quran shows that all nations, either ethnically Jewish or Gentile, will have salvation if they believe in Allah and are righteous:

"Lo! those who believe, and those who are Jews, and Sabaeans, and Christians whosoever believeth in Allah and the Last Day and doeth right there shall no fear come upon them neither shall they grieve." (Quran 5:69)

Hence, people are judged individually, rather than a nation. Furthermore, the Holy Quran confirms that Israel was favored and their prayers were answered as a nation but as in the Bible, fell from its favored status;

"And when there comes to them a Book from Allah, confirming what is with them,- although from of old they had prayed for victory against those without Faith,- when there comes to them that which they (should) have recognized, they refuse to believe in it but the curse of Allah is on those without Faith." (Quran 2:89)

94. Judah or Saul?

Errancy; Saul is promised to be the permanent king of Israel (1 Samuel 13:13) *Vs* The tribe of Judah is promised the permanent kingdom of Israel (Genesis 49:10)

Excuse; That is what it says but that is not what it means. What Samuel says is not a promise, only a hypothetical statement.

Rebuttal: Whether Saul's rein as king was temporary or permanent, the fact remains that Saul was an anointed king of Israel, thus breaking and contradicting the supposed everlasting rule by the tribe of Judah;

"Samuel also said unto Saul, The Lord sent me to anoint thee to be king over his people, over Israel: now therefore hearken thou unto the voice of the words of the Lord." (1 Samuel 15:1)

Correction: Allah in the Holy Quran clarifies that to be crowned as a humanly king is not permanent and that Allah can make or remove kings as He chooses:

"Their Prophet said unto them: Lo! Allah hath raised up Saul to be a king for you. They said: How can he have kingdom over us when we are more deserving of the kingdom than he is, since he hath not been given wealth enough? He said: Lo! Allah hath chosen him above you, and hath increased him abundantly in wisdom and stature. Allah bestoweth His sovereignty on whom He will. Allah is All Embracing, All Knowing." (Quran 2:247)

(VI.) WOMEN

95. Adam or Eve to blame?

Errancy; How does Eve, the mother of all human beings, measure in the Bible compared to the Quran? Assessing the Biblical depiction of Eve reveals the root of negative stereotyping towards women;

When God asked Adam why he ate from the forbidden tree, he answered, according to the Bible; "the Woman whom thou gavest to be with me, she gave me of the tree, and I did eat. And the Lord God said unto the woman, what is this that thou hast done? And the woman said, the serpent beguiled me, and I did eat." (Genesis 3:12-13)

"And I will put enmity between thee and the woman, and between thy seed and her seed; it shall bruise the head, and thou shalt bruise his heel. Unto the woman he (God) said, I will greatly multiply thy sorrow and thy conception; in sorrow thou shalt bring forth children; and thy desire shall be to thy husband, and he shall rule over thee." (Genesis 3:15-16)

As we can see in this scenario, Adam played a great part in committing the sin of eating from the forbidden tree, so why was it blamed on Eve?

Excuse; None available.

Correction: The Quran gives a non-biased narration, dispelling the gender inequality that the Bible portrays;

"Then did Satan make them slip from the (garden), and get them out of the state (of felicity) in which they had been. We said: "Get ye down, all (ye people), with enmity between yourselves. On earth will be your dwelling-place and your means of livelihood - for a time." (Quran 2:36)

"Then began Satan to whisper suggestions to them, bringing openly before their minds all their shame that was hidden from them (before): he said: "Your Lord only forbade you this tree, lest ye should become angels or such beings as live for ever."

"And he swore to them both, that he was their sincere adviser. So by deceit he brought about their fall: when they tasted of the tree, their shame became manifest to them, and they began to hide (by heaping) on themselves some of the leaves of the Garden."

"And their Lord called them, (saying): Did I not forbid you from that tree and tell you: Lo! Satan is an open enemy to you? They said: "Our Lord! We have wronged our own souls: If thou forgive us not and bestow not upon us Thy Mercy, we shall certainly be lost." (Quran 7:20-23)

In summary, while the Bible solely blames it on Eve, the Quran holds both Adam and Eve responsible and equally forgives both.

96. Adam and Eve equally punished?

Errancy; A disproportionate amount of Biblical wrath befell Eve in comparison to Adam. Malicious and agonizing punishments were thrust onto Eve, while the Bible maintains Adam's relative innocence.

In the Bible, Adam uses Eve as a scapegoat when interrogated by God;

"And the man said, the woman whom Thou gavest to be with me, she gave me of the tree, and I did eat." (Genesis 3:12) In turn, Eve blames the Serpent for hoaxing her.

Although Adam indirectly guiltily accuses God "Thou gavest to be with me", Eve is unfairly cursed four more times than Adam is. The four additional curses on Eve are delineated in Genesis;

"Unto the woman He said, (1st) I will greatly multiply thy sorrow and (2nd) thy conception; in sorrow thou shalt bring forth children; (3rd) and thy desire shall be to thy husband, and (4th) he shall rule over thee." (Genesis 3:16)

Adam's sin exceeded Eve's in the Biblical enactment because Adam succumbed to temptation quicker and through less influence than Eve endured with the serpent. Adam was reprimanded to a lesser degree, for a larger crime.

"Now the serpent was more subtle than any beast of the field which God had made." (Genesis 3:1)

Adam's scolding was a fraction to Eve's curses. The retributions placed on Adam were in fact additional damnations placed on Eve;

"And unto Adam he said, Because thou hast hearkened unto the voice of thy wife, and hast eaten of the tree, of which I commanded thee, saying, Thou shalt not eat of it: cursed is the ground for thy sake; (1st) in sorrow shalt thou eat of it all the days of thy life"

"Thorns also and thistles shall it bring forth to thee; (2nd)and thou shalt eat the herb of the field; In the sweat of thy face (3rd) shalt thou eat bread, till thou return unto the ground; for out of it wast thou taken: for dust thou art, and unto dust shalt thou return" (Genesis 3:17-19)

We recognize that Adam is given three in contrast to the four curses on Eve. Additional assessment reveals that Adam's dietary curses actually afflict Eve as well. Therefore, Eve suffers four separate curses and jointly shares Adam's three eating maledictions.

Paul in the Bible expounds on Eve's curses by saying; "...Adam was not deceived, but the woman was deceived and became a transgressor. Yet woman will be saved through bearing children" (1 Timothy 2:14-15)

Paul reiterates the Biblical perspective that Eve was debauched, hence women must suffer for retribution, while Adam, and men owe no supplementary penance.

Excuse; None available.

Correction: The Holy Quran counters the fallacious accusations placed on Eve;

"But Satan whispered evil to him: he said, "O Adam! shall I lead thee to the Tree of Eternity and to a kingdom that never decays?" In the result, they both ate of the tree, and so their nakedness appeared to them: both began to cover themselves with leaves of the garden, thus and Adam disobeyed his Lord, so went astray." (Quran 20:120-121)

The Quran expels the chauvinistic accusation that Eve was the lone perpetrator. The Quran also places Adam at the scene of the transgression and acknowledges he also spoke with Satan. Consequently, Adam and Eve were equally punished for their disobedience. In Conclusion, the women in the world are not indebted for any additional deeds towards Salvation, according to the Quran.

97. **Bible Forbids Women from Speaking**

Errancy; The Bible states: "The women should be silent in the churches, for they are not permitted to speak. Rather, let them be in submission, as in fact the law says. If they want to find out about something, they should ask their husbands at home." (1 Corinthians 14:34-35).

"Let the woman learn in silence with all subjection. But I suffer not a woman to teach, nor to usurp authority over the man, but to be in silence." (1 Timothy 2:11-15)

The Bible also forbids women from speaking in a church (1 Corinthians 14:34-35).

Excuse; That is what it says but that is not what it means. Apologetics assert that remaining silent in those verses actually meant being submissive. Otherwise, men and women are equally redeemed;

"there is neither male nor female; for you are all one in Christ Jesus" (Galatians 3:28)

Rebuttal: (See Reply letter [E] in Rebuttal Chart)

Paul obviously did not mean submissiveness when he said for women to be silent because in (1 Timothy 2:11) Paul says for women to be both submissive and silent, hence debunking the notion that Paul only meant submissive when he also stated for women to 'be silent' Again the apologetics try to twist the meanings of words by ignoring the context of the words used;

"But I suffer not a woman to teach" + "nor to usurp authority over the man." (1 Timothy 2:12)

The excuse actually shows how Paul contradicts himself and the Gospel even further, whereas in one instance Paul tells women to keep silent and in another instance, Paul foretells women prophesizing (Acts 2:17).

The apologetics err even further when they try to dig up passages where Paul likens men to women, in one passage Paul says women and men are saved equally (Galatians 3:28), while in another passage, Paul claims women have to stomach a different redemption;

"And Adam was not the one who was deceived; it was the woman who was deceived and became a sinner. But women will be saved through childbearing." (1 Timothy 2:14-15)

Correction: Within the Quran, you will not find a single verse that states a woman cannot speak during any particular time, let alone not at all! In fact, the Quran states the following:

"Indeed Allah has heard the statement of her that disputes with you (O Muhammad) concerning her husband and complains to Allah. And Allah hears the argument between you both. Verily Allah is All-Hearer, All Seer." (Quran 58:1)

Not only does this woman, Khaulah bint Tha'labah, speak with the Prophet (peace be upon him) but she is even arguing with him, and The Most Merciful, Allah, is listening to them both! The woman is not being condemned for speaking her mind and heart to the Prophet (peace be upon him) and disputing with him over a matter, yet instead, Allah is reassuring that he hears this woman's complaints and that He is the All-Hearer of all people, men, and women.

98. Female Amputation

Errancy; The Bible states that if two men were beating each other up, and the wife of one of them interfered, she should have her hand chopped off (Deuteronomy 25:11-12);

Excuse; 1st) the woman could have hurt the attacker's ability to have children by intentionally or accidentally hurting is genitals. 2nd) the woman was punished because she committed immodesty by touching another man's genitals

Rebuttal; 1st) This is a very pathetic excuse for cutting a woman's hand off, In fact, the same excuse can be used to justify the woman interfering for she could lose her husband's life if he were to get beaten up severely enough, and further more, if her hand was cut off, it would be her who would be left handicapped. Let us look even deeper into the reasons why the apologetics excuses are invalid for this unjust passage;

1st) If her hand is chopped off, she cannot hold her own children
2nd) The unjustly accused woman possibly saved her husband from also being hurt or killed.
3rd) Bravery and devotion to the husband is looked upon as a punishable act.

Hence, the first excuse is invalid because it can be reversed to justify the woman "interfering" with her husband being attacked.

2nd) The woman was not committing adultery because the act of touching another man was in the form of self-defense (protecting her husband) and in no way for foul purposes.

Correction: Nowhere in the Holy Quran is this horrid law repeated and even if the woman's intentions were ill willed, the Quran is not as severe as the Bible;

"The woman and the man guilty of adultery or fornication, - flog each of them with a hundred stripes: Let not compassion move you in their case, in a matter prescribed by Allah, if ye believe in Allah and the Last Day: and let a party of the Believers witness their punishment." (Quran 24:2)

99. Divorce Allowed?

Errancy; Divorce allowed (Deuteronomy 24:1–4) *Vs* Divorce not allowed (Mark 10:1–12) and (1 Corinthians 7:10–16)

Excuse; that is what it says but that is not what it means. Jesus and Paul were talking about what God wants yet Moses was talking about what actually happens.

Rebuttal: (See Reply letter [E] in Rebuttal Chart) The problem with this excuse is that Jesus does indeed acknowledge what Moses said and overrides it by saying Moses said this because of a fault within the Jews, but now this fault is punishable by death. The reason Moses allowed divorce is no longer acceptable to anyone;

"Whosoever shall put away his wife, and marry another, committeth adultery against her." (Mark 10:11)

"Whosoever", meaning anyone under any condition is not allowed to divorce their wife and visa versa, and if they do divorce their wife, the punishment is death because Jesus equated divorce with adultery and adultery is punishable by stoning to death.

Correction: In the Holy Quran, God understands that there are many conditions that warrant divorce. Spouses do not have to stay together under a death threat as it is claimed to be that Jesus said this in the Bible. Instead, two married people are allowed to divorce one another after they have attempted to reconcile their differences. God states within the Holy Quran that if a divorce is intended to take place, that each person wait 4 months before doing so, as a "waiting" or cooling off" period:

"For those who wish to separate from their wives, then they shall wait four months. If they concede, then God is most forgiving, merciful." (Quran 2:226)

"Once the interim is fulfilled, you may reconcile with them equitably, or go through with the separation equitably. You shall have two equitable witnesses witness the divorce before God. This is to enlighten those who believe in God and the Last Day. Anyone who reverences God, He will create an exit for him." (Quran 65:2)

At any moment during the 4-month interim the divorce may be retracted and the couple may settle their differences.

100. A Divorcee is an adulteress?

Errancy; A major problem in the Bible is the condemnation of divorcees. Once a woman has been with a man (in a marital relationship) the woman (now divorced) naturally desires to remarry, yet the Bible states that the marriage to a divorcee is punishable by death;

"Whosoever marries a divorced woman commits adultery." (Matthew 5:32)

Jesus equated divorce with adultery and adultery was punishable by stoning to death.

The Bible contradicts itself in this regard by wording in another section that women are ratified remarriage without repercussion; as Moses says a divorcee "may go and be another man's wife" (Deuteronomy 24:2)

Excuse; None available.

Correction: The Holy Quran corrects this degradation and contradiction within the Bible by stating that divorcees are not sinners, instead they are just as honorable as women whom have never been married, for marriage and divorce have no bearing on a woman's character and as such, these divorcees are to be treated in kindness as well as be given permission to remarry:

"A divorce is only permissible twice: after that, the parties should either hold Together on equitable terms, or separate with kindness. It is not lawful for you, (Men), to take back any of your gifts (from your wives), except when both parties fear that they would be unable to keep the limits ordained by Allah. If ye (judges) do indeed fear that they would be unable to keep the limits ordained by Allah, there is no blame on either of them if she give something for her freedom. These are the limits ordained by Allah; so do not transgress them if any do transgress the limits ordained by Allah, such persons wrong (Themselves as well as others).

"So if a husband divorces his wife (the third time), He cannot, after that, re-marry her until after she has married another husband and He has divorced her. In that case there is no blame on either of them if they re-unite, provided they feel that they can keep the limits ordained by Allah. Such are the limits ordained by Allah, which He makes plain to those who understand." (Quran 2:229-30)

101. Rekindling Love?

Errancy; Sometimes love can leave one's heart yet that same love can be rekindled again, yet the Bible does not allow this re-inflammation of the heart. A divorced woman who marries another man, and then divorces again, cannot return to her original love;

"And if the latter husband hate her, and write her a bill of divorcement, and giveth it in her hand, and sendeth her out of his house; or if the latter husband die, which took her to be his wife; Her former husband, which sent her away, may not take her again to be his wife, after that she is defiled; for that is abomination before the Lord: and thou shalt not cause the land to sin, which the Lord thy God giveth thee for an inheritance." (Deuteronomy 24:3-4)

Excuse; None available.

Correction: The Holy Quran does not call these two time divorced women defilements as is stated within the Bible, instead they are honorable women that can return home to their original loves:

"So if a husband divorces his wife (the third time), He cannot, after that, re-marry her until after she has married another husband and He has divorced her. In that case there is no blame on either of them if they re-unite; provided they feel that they can keep the limits ordained by Allah. Such are the limits ordained by Allah, which He makes plain to those who understand." (Quran 2:230)

102. Kicked out of the house?

Errancy; In another deviation within the Bible, a divorced woman is to be thrown out of her home (Deuteronomy 24:1)

"When a man hath taken a wife, and married her and it come to pass that she find no favor in his eyes, because he hath found some uncleanness in her: then let him write her a bill of divorcement, and give it in her hand, and send her out of his house."

It is a shameful punishment for a woman to be sent out of the home that her and her husband shared.

This manner of removing women from their former homes is repeated in the following passage;

"And if the latter husband hate her, and write her a bill of divorcement, and giveth it in her hand, and sendeth her out of his house" (Deuteronomy 24:3)

Excuse; None available.

Correction: The Holy Quran teaches us that a man has no right to send out a woman he has divorced from the home, leaving her to be homeless in the streets:

"O Prophet! When ye (men) divorce women, divorce them for their (legal) period and reckon the period, and keep your duty to Allah, your Lord. Expel them not from their houses nor let them go forth unless they commit open immorality. Such are the limits (imposed by) Allah; and whoso transgresseth Allah's limits, he verily wrongeth his soul. Thou knowest not: it may be that Allah will afterward bring some new thing to pass" (Quran 65:1)

103. Ex-husband's child?

Errancy; In the Bible, Moses is depicted to allow women to immediately remarry after a divorce (Deuteronomy 24:1-2). The error with this broad law is that if a woman immediately remarries, and is unknowingly pregnant, no one will know who the father of the baby is.

In contradiction to Moses, Jesus is falsely recorded to have said in the Bible;

"whoever marries a divorced woman commits adultery." (Matthew 5:32)

This was stated seemingly to prevent the spread of fatherless children

Excuse; None available.

Correction: The Holy Quran solves the problem of unknown fathers to children of divorcees as created in the Bible, without alienating and punishing the mothers to a life without remarriage as Jesus is claimed to do;

"Divorced women shall wait concerning themselves for three monthly periods. Nor is it lawful for them to hide what Allah Hath created in their wombs, if they have faith in Allah and the Last Day. And their husbands have the better right to take them back in that period, if they wish for reconciliation. And women shall have rights similar to the rights against them, according to what is equitable; but men have a degree (of advantage) over them. And Allah is Exalted in Power, Wise." (Quran 2:228)

In order for the identity of the child's father to be known, divorcees must wait 3 months before remarriage, to verify before marrying another whether or not they are pregnant. This method even eliminates today's method of men taking blood tests which leads to the ex-couples fighting and deeming this method to be inaccurate.

104. <u>Widows and Sisters do Not Inherit</u>

Errancy; In (Numbers 27:8-11), Moses describes the rules of inheritance that God presumably has stated. If a man dies, his son inherits the estate; his daughter gets nothing. Only if there is no son, then the daughter inherits. If there are no children, then the estate is given to the man's brothers and his sisters get nothing.

Excuse; None available.

Correction: The Quran abolished this male greediness;

"Unto the men (of a family) belongeth a share of that which parents and near kindred leave, and unto the women a share of that which parents and near kindred leave, whether it be little or much a legal share." (Quran 4:7)

"And unto you belongeth a half of that which your wives leave, if they have no child; but if they have a child then unto you the fourth of that which they leave, after any legacy they may have bequeathed, or debt (they may have contracted, hath been paid). And unto them belongeth the fourth of that which ye leave if ye have no child, but if ye have a child then the eighth of that which ye leave, after any legacy ye may have bequeathed, or debt (…ye may have contracted, hath been paid). And if a man or a woman have a distant heir (having left neither parent nor child), and he (or she) have a brother or a sister (only on the mother's side) then to each of them twain (the brother and the sister) the sixth, and if they be more than two, then they shall be sharers in the third, after any legacy that may have been bequeathed or debt (contracted) not injuring (the heirs by willing away more than a third of the heritage) hath been paid. A commandment from Allah. Allah is knower, Indulgent." (Quran 4:12)

105. Rapist must marry the victim

Errancy; "If a man happens to meet a virgin who is not pledged to be married and rapes her and they are discovered, he shall pay the girl's father fifty shekels of silver. He must marry the girl, for he has violated her. He can never divorce her as long as he lives" (Deuteronomy 22:28-30)

One must ask a simple question here, who is really being punished, the offender who raped the woman or the woman who was raped? According to the Bible, a woman must spend the rest of her life with the man who committed the treacherous crime of raping her.

Excuse; None available.

Correction: Whereas the voice of a woman is absent in the Bible, the Holy Quran enables women to be heard:

"O ye who believe! Ye are forbidden to inherit women against their will. Nor should ye treat them with harshness, that ye may take away part of the dower ye have given them,-except where they have been guilty of open lewdness; on the contrary live with them on a footing of kindness and equity. If ye take a dislike to them it may be that ye dislike a thing, and Allah brings about through it a great deal of good." (Quran 4:19)

The Prophet Muhammad (peace be upon him) Says in (Volume 9, Book 86, Number 101) Narrated by Aisha:" It is essential to have the consent of a woman (for the marriage)".

106. Married to the brother-in-law?

Errancy; Here is yet another case from the Bible where a woman is forced to marry someone without any consent in the matter;

"If brethren dwell together, and one of them die and have no child, the wife of the dead shall not marry without unto a stranger; her husband's brother shall go in unto her, and take her to him to wife." (Deuteronomy 25:5)

Excuse; None available.

Correction: Again, the Holy Quran lifts up the status of women as equals and important decision makers, as we see here, especially in their own marriage:

"O you who believe! You are forbidden to inherit women against their will, and you should not treat them with harshness, that you may take away part of the dower you have given them, unless they commit open illegal sexual intercourse. And live with them honorably. If you dislike them, it may be that you dislike a thing and Allah brings through it a great deal of good." (Quran 4:19)

107. Why wasn't Mary stoned to death ?

Errancy; A girl not found to be a virgin was to be killed (Deuteronomy 22:13- 21) According to the Bible, the punishment for adultery is death by stones:

"But if the thing is true, that the tokens of virginity were not found in the young woman, then they shall bring out the young woman to the door of her father's house, and the men of her city shall stone her to death with stones, because she has wrought folly in Israel by playing the harlot in her father's house; so you shall purge the evil from the midst of you." (Deuteronomy 22:20-21)

Why then was Mary's life spared by her community for apparently having a child with no apparent father?

Excuse; None available.

Correction: The Reason Mary was left to travel freely, proudly displaying her infant Jesus without being executed is explained in the Quran. The Holy Quran completes the missing puzzles often overlooked, ignored, or deliberately avoided by non-Muslim theologians.

We know from the Gospel, that even 30 years after the birth of Jesus, that stoning an adulterous woman was common. In (John 8), Jesus, as an adult, prevented a crowd from stoning a woman accused of adultery;

"They told him, "Teacher, we found this woman in adultery, in the very act. Now in our law, Moses commanded us to stone such women. What then do you say about her? They said this testing him, that they might have something to accuse him of.

But Jesus stooped down, and wrote on the ground with his finger. But when they continued asking him, he looked up and said to them, "He who is without sin among you, let him throw the first stone at her." (John 8:4-7)

Thirty Years earlier at the time of Jesus' birth, it would take a miracle to avert the Israelis from killing Mary, yet the Holy Quran reveals this rescuing miracle. When the Israelis approached Mary and her infant Jesus to question her and inquire about the fatherless child, something unexpected happened:

"Then she brought him to her people, carrying him. They said: "O Mary! Truly an amazing thing hast thou brought! O sister of Aaron! Thy father was not a wicked man nor was thy mother a harlot."

But she pointed to him. They said: "How should we speak to one who was a child in the cradle?"

He said: "I am indeed a servant of Allah: He hath given me revelation and made me a prophet; and He hath made me blessed wheresoever I be, and hath enjoined on me Prayer and Charity as long as I live; (He) hath made me kind to my mother, and not overbearing or miserable" (Quran 19:27-32)

In conclusion, after witnessing the miracle of God, (the newborn Messiah praising God), Mary's innocence was confirmed. Interestingly, As Jesus had this previous experience of stopping the stoning of a suspected adulterous as an infant; thirty years later, Jesus again persuaded a crowd to avoid stoning a alleged adulterous in the Gospel of John, chapter 8.

108. After Birth?

Errancy; Women who have given birth to a boy are ritually unclean for 40 days. If the baby is a girl, the mother is unclean for 80 days. (Leviticus 12:1-5)

This monstrous saying shows that giving birth to a girl is twice as polluting as is giving birth to a boy.

Excuse; None available.

Correction: In Islam, the birth of a daughter is equal to a birth of a son; the Holy Quran corrects the perception in the Bible that the birth of a daughter is more polluted or evil than the birth of a son. God reiterates for us what evil men used to do:

"When news is brought to one of them, of (the birth of) a female (child), his face darkens, and he is filled with inward grief!"

"With shame does he hide himself from his people, because of the bad news he has had! Shall he retain it on (sufferance and) contempt, or bury it in the dust? Ah! what an evil (choice) they decide on?" (Quran 16:58-59)

Hence, female children are not shameful or dirtier than male children are, in fact, both births are equal:

"To Allah belongs the dominion of the heavens and the earth. He creates what He wills (and plans). He bestows (children) male or female according to His Will (and Plan)," (Quran 42:49)

Hence, a birth of a girl or a boy is equal blessings from God.

109. Birth of a Daughter is a loss

Errancy; Many Catholics consider the birth of a daughter to be a great loss. In the Catholic Bible, Apocrypha, Book of Ecclesiasticus, it says, "The Birth of a Daughter is a loss" (Ecclesiastics 22:3).

Excuse; None available.

Correction: God clarifies within the Quran, in His guidance to all of humanity that boys and girls are born equal and that those who assume that having a daughter is a shameful loss are wrong:

"When news is brought to one of them, of (the birth of) a female (child), his face darkens, and he is filled with inward grief!"

"With shame does he hide himself from his people, because of the bad news he has had! Shall he retain it on (sufferance and) contempt, or bury it in the dust? Ah! what an evil (choice) they decide on?" (Quran 16:58-59)

Hence, female children are not less than male children are, in fact, both births are equal:

"To Allah belongs the dominion of the heavens and the earth. He creates what He wills (and plans). He bestows (children) male or female according to His Will (and Plan)," (Quran 42:49)

110. Widow can't marry a priest?

Errancy; In a further affront on a widow's dignity, priests are forbidden for marriage. In the Bible, widows are grouped together with harlots as women forbidden for matrimony to a priest;

"A widow, or a divorced woman, or profane, or an harlot, these shall he (the priest) not take: but he shall take a virgin of his own people to wife." (Leviticus 21:14)

Excuse; None available.

Correction: The Holy Quran clarifies that all believers are allowed to marry a widow:

"If any of you die and leave widows behind, they shall wait concerning themselves four months and ten days: When they have fulfilled their term, there is no blame on you if they dispose of themselves in a just and reasonable manner. And Allah is well acquainted with what ye do."

"And there is no blame on you respecting that which you speak indirectly in the asking of (such) women in marriage or keep (the proposal) concealed within your minds; Allah knows that you win mention them, but do not give them a promise in secret unless you speak in a lawful manner, and do not confirm the marriage tie until the writing is fulfilled, and know that Allah knows what is in your minds, therefore beware of Him, and know that Allah is Forgiving, Forbearing." (Quran 2:234-235)

111. Divorced Women can't marry a priest

Errancy; In a further affront on a divorcee's dignity, these women are forbidden marriage with priests. In the Bible, divorcees are grouped together with harlots as women whom are forbidden for matrimony to a priest;

"A widow, or a divorced woman, or profane, or a harlot, these shall he (the priest) not take: but he shall take a virgin of his own people to wife." (Leviticus 21:14)

Excuse; None available.

Correction: A divorced woman in the Quran can marry anyone, including her ex-husband. Believers can even marry the women divorced from pagans;

"O ye who believe! When believing women come unto you as fugitives, examine them. Allah is best aware of their faith. Then, if ye know them for true believers, send them not back unto the disbelievers. They are not lawful for the disbelievers, nor are the disbelievers lawful for them. And give the disbelievers that which they have spent (upon them). And it is no sin for you to marry such women when ye have given them their dues." (Quran 60:10)

112. Who are Eve's parent?

Errancy; According to the Christian's logic regarding the relationship of Jesus to God, children who are born with only one parent must have God as the other parent. This argument would be logical except for the fact that Eve, who only had one parent, is not considered the daughter of God as Jesus is considered the son of God.

The similarities between Jesus and Eve are almost identical;

(Mary's womb was barren and childless similar to Adam's rib, childless and barren.) and (Adam's rib made Eve and Mary's womb made Jesus.)

Excuse; None available.

Correction: The womb and the rib were used as a tool by Allah to Create.

Eve was born from another human as Jesus was born from another human; Jesus was born with the help of Allah as Eve was born with the help of Allah. Allah creates, and does not beget.

"There is no god but He: It is He Who gives life and gives death, - The Lord and Cherisher to you and your earliest ancestors." (Quran 44:8)

"He begetteth not nor was begotten." (Quran 112:3)

"The similitude of Jesus before Allah is as that of Adam; He created him from dust, then said to him: "Be". And he was." (Quran 3:59)

113. Selling a Woman?

Errancy; Women are not property, except in the Bible (Exodus 21:7-11) A father can sell a daughter into slavery to pay a debt. A daughter sold into slavery is not released at the end of six years as is an ordinary male slave.

Excuse; None available.

Correction: Fortunately, for all of us, God gave us our rights and freedom in the Quran over 1400 years ago. We do not have to be enslaved to the laws of the Bible:

God says: "O ye who believe! Ye are forbidden to inherit women against their will. Nor should ye treat them with harshness, that ye may Take away part of the dower ye have given them,-except where they have been guilty of open lewdness; on the contrary live with them on a footing of kindness and equity. If ye take a dislike to them it may be that ye dislike a thing, and Allah brings about through it a great deal of good." (Quran 4:19)

Regarding a parent's debt or poverty, we are commanded in the Quran not to slay children to alleviate poverty:

"Say: Come I will recite what your Lord has forbidden to you- (remember) that you do not associate anything with Him and show kindness to your parents, and do not slay your children for (fear of) poverty - We provide for you and for them" (Quran 6:151)

114. Men Worth More?

Errancy; Again, the Bible tries to propagate a disproportionate value between men and women;

"If your valuation is of the male from twenty years even to sixty years old, then your valuation shall be fifty shekels of silver, after the shekel of the sanctuary. 'Or if it is a female, then your valuation shall be thirty shekels." (Leviticus 27:3-4)

Excuse; None available.

Correction: The Holy Quran corrects all of these disproportionate values between men and women by stating that both are equal blessings from God:

"To Allah belongs the dominion of the heavens and the earth. He creates what He wills (and plans). He bestows (children) male or female according to His Will (and Plan)," (Quran 42:49)

115. Chastity

Errancy; A betrothed virgin who is seduced in the city is to be put to death unless she cries for help. (Deuteronomy 22:23-24)

This is an unreliable way to judge whether a woman is in pain or not, for what if she is not heard verbally? To rely on external indicators to make a judgment of death is quite harsh. Is God not a merciful God?

Excuse; None available.

Correction: The Quran teaches all of us that God knows what is the truth in the seen and the unseen, the heard and the silent and He will judge accordingly for God has mercy over all, no verbal plea for help needs to be heard for God to know the guilty and the innocent:

"Seest thou not that Allah doth know (all) that is in the heavens and on earth? There is not a secret consultation between three, but He makes the fourth among them, - Nor between five but He makes the sixth, - nor between fewer nor more, but He is in their midst, wheresoever they be: In the end will He tell them the truth of their conduct, on the Day of Judgment. For Allah has full knowledge of all things." (Quran 58:7)

On the matter of rape:

"Those who cannot afford to get married shall maintain morality until God provides for them from His grace. Those among your servants who wish to be freed in order to marry, you shall grant them their wish, once you realize that they are honest. And give them from God's money that He has bestowed upon you. You shall not force your servant girls to commit prostitution, seeking the materials of this world, if they wish to be chaste. If anyone forces them, then God, seeing that they are forced, is Forgiver, Merciful." (Quran 24:33)

116. Pagan Wives?

Errancy; Divorce pagan wives (Ezra 10:11) *Vs* Do not divorce pagan wives (1 Corinthians 7:12).

Excuse; 1st) Later Scripture replaces Previous Scripture. 2nd) not all pagans are the same.

Rebuttal: 1st) (See Reply letter [G] in Rebuttal Chart). 2nd) Either you do believe in God or you don't, or as the Christians say; either your saved or not.

Correction: The Quran clarifies that men are not allowed to be married to pagan women:

"Do not marry unbelieving women (idolaters), until they believe: A slave woman who believes is better than an unbelieving woman, even though she allures you. Nor marry (your girls) to unbelievers until they believe: A man slave who believes is better than an unbeliever, even though he allures you. Unbelievers do (but) beckon you to the Fire. But Allah beckons by His Grace to the Garden (of bliss) and forgiveness, and makes His Signs clear to mankind: That they may celebrate His praise." (Quran 2:221)

The Holy Quran settles the difference in the Bible by stating that men are not allowed to marry pagans/atheists but we are allowed to marry believers in the God of Abraham:

"This day are (all) things good and pure made lawful unto you. The food of the People of the Book is lawful unto you and yours is lawful unto them. (Lawful unto you in marriage) are (not only) chaste women who are believers, but chaste women among the People of the Book, revealed before your time, - when ye give them their due dowers, and desire chastity, not lewdness, nor secret intrigues if any one rejects faith, fruitless is his work, and in the Hereafter he will be in the ranks of those who have lost (all spiritual good)." (Quran 5:5)

117. Maiden Names?

Errancy; The Bible teaches that a woman must lose her life long father's last name upon marriage;

The elimination of the wife's family name is made clear by (Genesis 2:23), "...she shall be called woman because she was taken out of man."

As well as (Genesis 5:2) "Male and female created he them: and blessed them, and called their name Adam."

Excuse; None available.

Correction: In the Muslim World, women have the option to keep their father's last name:

"Call them by (the names of) their fathers: that is juster in the sight of Allah. But if ye know not their father's (names, call them) your Brothers in faith, or your maulas. But there is no blame on you if ye make a mistake therein: (what counts is) the intention of your hearts: and Allah is Oft-Returning, Most Merciful." (Quran 33:5)

(VII.) JESUS

118. Two Blind Men?

Errancy; Jesus heals two blind men on the way to Jericho. (Matthew 20:29-34) *Vs* He heals one blind man. (Mark 10:46-52)

Excuse; That is what it says but that is not what it means; Although Mark says one, he could have meant two.

Rebuttal: (See Reply letter [E] in Rebuttal Chart). Curing one blind person may have been coincidental, curing two is an absolute miracle, and for Mark to ignore the second time a man was supposedly cured or just focus on one and ignore the other is the similitude of a person ignoring the sun being eclipsed.

Furthermore, in other situations where there were two individuals, Mark mentions "both";

"And with him they crucify two thieves; the one on his right hand, and the other on his left." (Mark 15:27)
Correction: The Quran clarifies that Jesus was given the power by God to heal all blind people, and hence, Jesus could have healed more than one or two people, for he had that power God bestowed upon him to heal people (plural).

"and thou (Jesus) healest those born blind, and the lepers, by My leave." (Quran 5:110)

119. Some Sick?

Errancy; Jesus healed all that were sick. (Matthew 8:16, Luke 4:40) *Vs* Jesus healed many (but not all). (Mark 1:32-34)

Excuse; None available.

Correction: According to the Holy Quran, Jesus healed those present; therefore not erring as in the Bible by claiming absolutely everyone who was sick was healed, hence settling whether all or some were healed:

"Then will Allah say: "O Jesus the son of Mary! Recount My favor to thee and to thy mother. Behold! I strengthened thee with the holy spirit, so that thou didst speak to the people in childhood and in maturity. Behold! I taught thee the Book and Wisdom, the Law and the Gospel and behold! thou makest out of clay, as it were, the figure of a bird, by My leave, and thou breathest into it and it becometh a bird by My leave, and thou healest those born blind, and the lepers, by My leave. And behold! thou bringest forth the dead by My leave. And behold! I did restrain the Children of Israel from (violence to) thee when thou didst show them the clear Signs, and the unbelievers among them said: 'This is nothing but evident magic'." (Quran 5:110)

The Quran clarifies that the correct answer to whether Jesus cured many or all people is that he cured (many) because technically, there may have been some sick with a cold or flu which did not come forward to be healed, so Jesus did not cure (all) as the Quran confirms for Jesus indeed was given the power to cure some types of sicknesses but not every ones sickness.

120. Beyond a Reasonable Doubt

Errancy; In the next twenty ways, the Quran corrects the Bible in regards to the claimed crucifixion of Jesus and here we will witness one of the phenomenal expansive statements that covers and resolves an entire episode.

The Quran demystifies the disorder in the Bible surrounding the crucifixion of Jesus. For over 2,000 years, the Bible editors have been stressed to harmonize the following eighteen tensions that the Quran relieves with one single verse.

Like a Judge, deciding a murder case, Allah, through the Quran, debunks the presumptive evidence in the Bible by stating there is a reasonable doubt. Listed in chronological order are the eighteen claims of the Bible preceding the judgment in the Quran;

Allegations answered?

Jesus answers no charges at his hearing before Pilate. (Matthew 27:11-14) *Vs* Jesus answers all charges at his hearing before Pilate. (John 18:33-37)

Excuse; None available.

Correction: (Continued from 120-140)

121. Too Heavy?

Errancy; Who bore the cross? They compelled Simon to bear the cross of Jesus. (Matthew 27:32), (Luke 23:26) & (Mark 15:21) *Vs* Jesus was bearing the cross himself. (John 19:17)

Excuse; Bible proponents pursue to rationalize this disparity by proposing Jesus collapsed after the flogging and interrogation, at which point Simon persistent to carry the cross. The problem with this assumed scenario is more questions than answers arise.

Rebuttal: First, if Jesus did indeed fall, and did not carry the cross, why didn't any of the disciples document the "fall of Jesus"? Second, if John did indeed delete the detail of Jesus being too decrepit, in order to demonstrate divinity; doubt develops regarding what other erasures have taken place discrediting the deity of Jesus? While on the other hand, it is only in the testimony of John do we find derogatory statements suggesting Jesus is divine. Third, less minor details are mentioned in the Gospel of John, i.e. (the exact hour Jesus was placed on the cross John 19:14), etc... How then could the occurrence of a fellow disciple (Simon), participating in the crucifixion of Jesus be disregarded?

We realize the suggestion that the disciple John "left out" this occurrence is unacceptable, casting an even larger shadow of distrust on John's Biblical narration.

Correction: (Continued from 120-140)

122. What did they put Jesus on?

Errancy; In (Mark 15: 32) we are told that Jesus was put on a "cross" to be crucified:

"Let Christ the King of Israel descend now from the cross, that we may see and believe. And they that were crucified with him reviled him."

The word used here for "cross" in the Greek edition is "stauros", yet in (1 Peter 2:24) we are told that Jesus was crucified on the "tree":

"Who his own self bare our sins in his own body on the tree, that we, being dead to sins, should live unto righteousness: by whose stripes ye were healed."

The word in this verse for "tree" in the Greek edition is "xulon"

Excuse; Bible proponents pursue to rationalize this disparity by proposing a mistranslation from the Greek text, but as we witnessed, even the verses in Greek use differing words to describe the wooden object allegedly used to defeat Jesus. Yes, both a tree and a cross can be equally used as a stake, stick, staff, for all words are related in the lexicon meaning of the two, yet this relationship does not excuse the fact that two different words were used. A tree and a cross can also have completely opposite dictionary meanings. Hence, showing an equal degree of difference in the meanings.

Rebuttal: First, suggesting a mistranslation of the Bible from Greek is unacceptable because Christians claim the Bible is divine and that the Bible is the exact word of God in every language. Second, both the words used in Greek are themselves divergent and their meanings are not identical. Third, such an explanation tries to bridge elements from their primal to their completed state, which is a long process absent between the passages. For example "he was killed with a rock" or "he was killed with a sculpture", two contradictory weapons, depicting unreliable witnesses.

Correction: (Continued from 120-140)

123. My Father or Abba?

Errancy; What did Jesus call God while allegedly on the cross? "My Father" (Matthew 26:39) *Vs* "Abba" (Mark 14:36)

Excuse; Mistranslation.

Rebuttal: (See Reply letter [F] in Rebuttal Chart)

Correction: (Continued from 120-140)

124. Final Prayer?

Errancy; There is a riddle regarding the last words before the reputed crucifixion. Did Jesus indeed pray to God to prevent the excruciation?

"And going a little farther he fell on his face and prayed, "My Father, if it be possible, let this cup pass from me; nevertheless, not as I will, but as thou wilt." (Matthew 26:39)

Here we see Jesus was praying to be saved;

"And he said, "Abba, Father, all things are possible to thee; remove this cup from me; yet not what I will, but what thou wilt." (Mark 14:36)

"Father, if thou art willing, remove this cup from me; nevertheless not my will, but thine, be done." (Luke 22:42)

The major problem lies in John's testimony;

"Now is my soul troubled. And what shall I say? 'Father, save me from this hour'? No, for this purpose I have come to this hour." (John 12:27)

Jesus denies he will pray to be saved

Note; the quote in the narration of John is during the Passover Festival at the Temple in Jerusalem, before the trial by Pharisees.

The key problem here is that John portrays Jesus both denying he will pray and actually omitting the prayer of Jesus during the crucifixion. In (John 19:16-30), there is no prayer as the other three disciples documented. Instead, a strong and silent Jesus is illustrated.

We conclude that based the four stories; there is a web of lies. If we start from the first three pupils and compare them with Jesus in the gospel of John denying he will pray for salvation, then all three made a false testimony. Yet if all three actually did see Jesus ask for deliverance, then John was the false witness because he claimed Jesus would not make the plea and disregarded the wish when it was made. This is an ongoing bolstering attempt by John, characterizing a Jesus that can lift the cross by himself without the help of Simon and does not need God's help either while on the cross.

Excuse; Apologetics say that Jesus nobly yet unenthusiastically faced death.

Rebuttal: The problem with this excuse is that John claims Jesus did eagerly face death because that was his whole purpose for being, Jesus was waiting his whole life for that moment and was not about to spoil it by asking to be saved;

"Now is my soul troubled. And what shall I say? 'Father, save me from this hour'? No, for this purpose I have come to this hour." (John 12:27)

Jesus is not troubled and claims he will not even ask for being rescued, so again we have a brave Jesus in the Gospel of John, while we have a

Jesus who was not only unenthusiastic to face death, a Jesus who eagerly avoided death in the other three Gospels.

Correction: (Continued from 120-140)

125. The last word?

Errancy; Another alteration is the alleged last words of Jesus before he died;

"Father, into thy hands I commit my spirit!" (Luke 23:46) *Vs* "It is finished" (John 19:30).

Excuse; 1st) Bible proponents pursue to rationalize this disparity by proposing the proximity of the two disciples distorted their descriptions. 2nd) Another attempted explanation is that Luke used the last words that he felt were necessary for his gospel account, which concentrated on the humanity of Jesus. While John, under duress, twisted the words of Jesus for the fulfillment of the salvific message.

Rebuttal: 1st) This is excusable for two witnesses of a traffic accident giving opposing accounts due to where they observed the event from. Yet it is unacceptable to excuse differing accounts between Bible authors asserting they are documenting the words of God. 2nd) This claim posses more questions than answers, similar to John deleting who carried the cross.

The intentional adding, deleting, or altering of the words or actions of Jesus to appease one's own personnel interpretation of the character of Jesus is blasphemy and should therefore be named "Luke's or John's opinion of the Bible", rather than "the Bible". For instead of having an actual recording, we are left with conjectures, hypotheses, and as the Bible defenders admit, self-satisfying alterations. In conclusion, the distinction shows a lack of respect on both authors, trading the precise presumed last dieing words of Jesus in exchange for their own gluttony.

Correction: (Continued from 120-140)

126. What did they give Jesus to drink?

Errancy; They gave him wine mingled with myrrh to drink. (Mark 15:23) *Vs* They gave him vinegar mingled with gall to drink. (Matthew 27:34)

Excuse; 1st) Bible proponents pursue to rationalize this disparity by proposing two different drinks were given to Jesus at two different times.

2nd) Another propagated explanation is that the myrrh and gall were mixed together.

Rebuttal: 1st) Though this is a hopeful explanation, it does not fit the text. Here are the verses in order from Matthew and Mark and including both times Jesus was given the drink;

Matthew	Mark
From the start of the crucifixion;	

27:34 - "they gave Him wine to drink mingled with gall; and after tasting it, He was unwilling to drink."
   (Greek "wine" is "ozos" which is a mixture of sour wine or vinegar and water.)
	15:23 "And they tried to give Him wine mixed with myrrh; but He did not take it."
	   (Greek "wine" is "oinos" which means simply, wine.)

several hours later	

27:48, "And immediately one of them ran, and taking a sponge, he filled it with sour wine, and put it on a reed, and gave Him a drink."
   (Greek "sour wine" is "ozos" or vinegar as above).
	15:36 "And someone ran and filled a sponge with sour wine, put it on a reed, and gave Him a drink."
	   (Greek "sour wine" is "ozos" or vinegar).

Therefore, the "different drinks at different times excuse" is only valid if we are examining only one disciple's testimony. 2nd) Parallel inspection refutes this mixing excuse because we still see that different drinks were given between Mark and Matthew.

This is another invalid justification because the mixture of the two is not mentioned, whereas mixtures are specified in other parts of the Bible;

"They that tarry long at the wine; they that go to seek mixed wine." (Proverbs 23:30)

"Thy silver is become dross, thy wine mixed with water: (Isaiah 1:22) etc…

Therefore, if the wine was mixed with anything, even as basic as water, it would have been mentioned. In conclusion, if the myrrh was already included to improve the smell of the wine, it would not have been mentioned separately in Mark, and if Mark saw fit to be detailed enough to mention the myrrh, then he would have certainly mentioned the secreted gall.

Correction: (Continued from 120-140)

127. <u>Two Mocking Thieves?</u>

Errancy; How many thieves on the cross mocked Jesus?

"Let the Christ, the King of Israel, come down now from the cross, that we may see and believe." Those who were crucified with him also reviled him." (Mark 15:32)

Both hanging thieves ridiculed Jesus

"One of the criminals who were hanged railed at him, saying, "Are you not the Christ? Save yourself and us!" But the other rebuked him, saying, "Do you not fear God, since you are under the same sentence of condemnation?" (Luke 23:39-40).

Only one thief ridiculed and the other defended Jesus

Excuse; Bible proponents pursue to rationalize this disparity by proposing the reader be less literalistic or accurate, instead they suggest we have an imaginative interpretation. The fictitious scenario we are requested to swallow is that both thieves mocked Jesus at first, and then one repented.

Rebuttal: We know this is a false rationale because if one of the thieves did indeed repent, then the remorse would have been documented as the Gospels record the repenting centurion standing below Jesus;

"and when the centurion, who stood facing him, saw that he thus breathed his last, he said; 'Truly this man was the Son of God!' (Mark 15:39) and (Matthew 27:54)

"Now when the centurion saw what had taken place, he praised God, and said, "Certainly this man was innocent!" (Luke 23:47)

Throughout the Bible, if a repent happened, especially in the presence of Jesus, it is recorded, therefore if they did not happen; they are not recorded as in the case of the criminal.

Another problem with this Luke inclined sequence is that it polarizes Mark even more. In Mark, who states both criminals taunted Jesus, then records a helpless Jesus crying twice and being teased till death by a third bystander (Mark 15:36) is in contrast to the prophetic Jesus in Luke.

While three spectators mocked a crying Jesus until his final hour in Mark, Luke documents a rebuke by the other thief who was silent up until then. This refutation by the thief then leads to an honorable predictive (yet untimely) monolog by Jesus disregarded in Mark "And he said to him, "Truly, I say to you, today you will be with me in Paradise." (Luke 23:43)

In conclusion, the more we examine the dialogs on the cross, the more diversity we see. We go from two mocking thieves and two cries in Mark to one mocking thief, and one cry. Therefore, we see a difference larger than a presumed repenting, which apparently did not take place.

Correction: (Continued from 120-140)

128. <u>See You in Heaven</u>

Errancy; a premature promise to paradise [Friday] was the day pledged to the partnering prisoner (Luke 23:43), yet on [Sunday] Jesus states he has not yet gone to Heaven (John 20:17).

Excuse; 1st) the time period peculiarity between Friday and Sunday is often blamed on punctuation between Greek and English, further insulting our Producer by pretending God took part in improper pronunciations. 2nd) That is what it says but that is not what it means. The Spirit of Jesus went immediately to Heaven but his body did not.

Rebuttal: 1st) the excuse of a mistranslation or mis-punctuation is unacceptable in the Light of the beautiful and authentic Quran (See Reply letter [I] in Rebuttal Chart).

2nd) If Jesus meant his body had not gone up yet, then he would have specified his body instead of stating "I" (as a whole) has not gone to the Father yet. The Gospel speaks of the body over 120 times;

"thy whole body should be cast into hell." (Matthew 5:29)

Jesus differentiates between himself and his body often;

"This is my body which is given for you" (Luke 22:19)

So it is inexcusable that he does not mention or does not specify that only his body did not see God yet as the Bible defenders assert.

Another reason why the (spirit only) excuse is faulty is that according to Christians, Jesus was God, so their spirit was already together, therefore there was no reason for the spirit only to ascend, and their supposed full reunion was on Sunday as Jesus states.

The third reason this excuse is invalid is that it would be accusing Jesus of being a liar! If his inner self (soul/spirit) already ascended to God and came back, then Jesus would be a liar to say, "I have not yet ascended to My Father".

Correction: (Continued from 120-140)

129. When did the curtain fall?

Errancy; Did Jesus die before the curtain of the temple was torn?

Yes (Matthew 27:50-51; Mark 15:37-38) *Vs* No (Luke 23:45-46).

Excuse; Luke wrote the events in reverse order.

Rebuttal: This is a selective rational, while disregarding that the rest of Luke's Gospel is not written in reverse order. Therefore, we cannot accept that just this part is in reverse to pardon the contradiction and ignore the rest of Luke's chronological order.

Correction: (Continued from 120-140)

130. The hours?

Errancy; Was Jesus on the cross at the sixth hour (Mark 15:33) *Vs* (John 19:14) In Pilate's court at the sixth hour.

Also

"It was the third hour, and they crucified him." (Mark 15:25) *Vs* "It was the sixth hour, and he was not yet crucified" (John 19:14)

Excuse; Matthew, Mark, and Luke) used a different system of numbering the hours of day (Hebrew) opposed to John (Roman).

Rebuttal: First, John was just as Jewish as the other three Gospels. Naturally, they would all use the same time format. For example, Americans all use "miles" to measure distance, and would not use "kilometers".

Second, it appears that John was not using a different time format, instead a different (time zone). While it was still daytime in the other Gospels (Mark 14:12-17), it was night time for John;

"He then having received the sop went immediately out: and it was night." (John 13:30)

Third, to appease to apologetics, we will assume for a moment that John did use the Roman time format. What the Christians ignore is that the Romans divided the night into four 3-hour watches, whereas the Jewish format divided the night into three 4-hour watches.

(Matthew 14:25) "And in the fourth watch of the night, he [Jesus] came to them, walking upon the sea."

(Mark 6:48) also says, "fourth watch", both indications that Matthew and Mark used the Roman format too. Therefore, if John used the Roman format, so did Matthew and Mark, which proves the discrepancy exists.

Fourth, Christian scholars disagree that the error comes from a difference between the Roman and Jewish time format;

According to the *Adam Clarke Commentary* (Mark 15:25), the passage (John 19:14) should read "the third hour" and that a manuscript error is involved.

Correction: (Continued from 120-140)

131. Eulogy?

Errancy; "and when the centurion, who stood facing him, saw that he thus breathed his last, he said, "Truly this man was the Son of God!" (Mark 15:39) and (Matthew 27:54) *Vs* "Now when the centurion saw what had taken place, he praised God, and said; "Certainly this man was innocent!" (Luke 23:47)

Excuse; Mistranslation.

Rebuttal: (See Reply letter [I] in Rebuttal Chart)

Correction: (Continued from 120-140)

132. Confirmation of Death?

Errancy; Joseph of Arimathea asks Pilate for Jesus' body, and Pilate is unaware of whether he is dead; only after sending a centurion and receiving this confirmation does he allow Joseph to take the body. (Mark 15:43-45) *Vs* Pilate actually authorizes the leg breaking to ensure they have all died and then authorizes Joseph to remove the body. (John 19:31-33, 38)

Excuse; None available.

Correction: (Continued from 120-140)

133. Cross Inscription?

Errancy; What was the exact wording on the cross?

"This is Jesus the King of the Jews" (Matthew 27:37) *Vs* "The King of the Jews" (Mark 15:26) *Vs* "This is the King of the Jews" (Luke 23:38) *Vs* "Jesus of Nazareth, the King of the Jews" (John 19:19).

Excuse; Mistranslation.

Rebuttal: (See Reply letter [I] in Rebuttal Chart)

Correction: (Continued from 120-140)

134. Nights of Burial?

Errancy; Jesus to be buried for three days and nights (Matthew 12:40) *Vs* Jesus buried for one day and two nights (Mark 15:42, 43, John 20:1)

Excuse; That is what it says but that is not what it means. Bible scholars stretch far to try to rectify this problem. These Bible scholars go as far as saying that a day in this particular verse does not mean a full 24 hour day.

Rebuttal: (See Reply letter [E] in Rebuttal Chart). What the apologetics are not grasping is that whether a day is shortened or extended by a day, one of the two conflicting verses will still be inconsistent with the other;

If one day equals to 12 hours instead of 24, then there is still a conflict with (Matthew 12:40) who says 3 days while (John 20:1) says 1. And if we were to extend the days, the same conflict would remain. If we are expected to believe a day is shorter in one verse, then consequently we have to shorten the days in the entire Bible; which would cause the 1 *Vs* 3 days problem to still be there.

Correction: (Continued from 120-140)

135. Spiced Wrap?

Errancy; Jesus' body wrapped in spices before the burial (John 19:39-40) *Vs* Jesus was only wrapped in a linen shroud and the spices were prepared after the burial (Mark 16: 1)

Excuse; (Mark 16:1) is speaking of adding extra spices and did not mention the spices that were surely already there.

Rebuttal: Actually, being buried in spice is an imperative part of Jewish burial customs so it would be imprudent to claim Mark did not mention it when he mentioned other trivial minute items such as the spice in Jesus' drink (Mark 15:23). Furthermore, Mark does not say "extra spice"; instead, the Gospel of Mark plainly says "spice".

Correction: (Continued from 120-140)

136. Who told?

Errancy; A young man in a white robe told the women where Jesus was (Mark 16:5) *Vs* "Two men . . . in dazzling apparel" later described as angels (Luke 24:4 and 24:23). *Vs* Mary met no one and returned saying, "They have taken the Lord out of the tomb, and we do not know where they have laid him" (John 20:2).

Excuse; Mary Magdalene having seen the tomb opened (John 20:1); she returned to tell the disciples, while the other two women at the tomb went in and saw the angels.

Rebuttal: Actually, the apologetics are ignoring the fact that the women saw the angel roll away the rock (Matthew 28:2-5) so if Mary Magdalene saw the tomb open, they inescapably saw the angel open the tomb as the other two saw (how can someone miss seeing an angel moving a boulder?) unless the accounts are inaccurate.

Correction: (Continued from 120-140)

137. Touched?

Errancy; Mary and the other women met Jesus on their way back from their first and only visit to the tomb. They took hold of his feet and worshipped him (Matthew 28:9) *Vs* Mary met Jesus on her second visit to the tomb Mary met Jesus just outside the tomb. When she saw Jesus, she did not recognize him. She mistook him for the gardener. She still thinks that Jesus' body is laid to rest somewhere and she demands to know where. However, when Jesus said her name she at once recognized him and called him "Teacher". Jesus said to her, "Do not hold me . . ." (John 20:11-17).

Excuse; Only men's testimonies were legal in the first century, thus, we have incomplete accounts, not all of the women's testimonies were recorded because they were not legally legitimate in those days.

Rebuttal: Then why record it at all in the Bible and causing discrepancies? The accounts are not only incomplete, they are inaccurate. One account tells of Jesus being touched, held, and worshiped and the other tells of Jesus not even being recognized and instructing not to be touched.

Correction: (Continued from 120-140)

138. Allowing Jesus to die?

Errancy; Jesus was rescued from death as an infant (Matthew 2:13), and Jesus rescued himself on a few occasions (John 7:1, John 8:59, John 12:36-37), why then wasn't Jesus rescued from the cross?

Excuse; It was not his time yet;

"Then they sought to take him: but no man laid hands on him, because his hour was not yet come." (John 7:30)

Rebuttal: There is no chronological significance in the alleged crucifixion date. In fact, if it were to have sacrificial credit, it was supposed to be done when Jesus was a child (Exodus 12:5);

"You may choose either a sheep or a goat, but it must be a one-year-old male without any defects."

Correction: (Continued from 120-140)

139. Different Bodies?

Errancy; Jesus appeared in a different body after the resurrection (Mark 16:12) *Vs* Jesus did not appear in a different body after the resurrection (Luke 24:34)

Excuse; copyist error. (Mark 16:9-20) is not found in many ancient manuscripts.

Rebuttal: (See Reply letter [F] in Rebuttal Chart).

Correction: Bible scholars confirm that their eyes were made to see a different person rather than Jesus (Luke 24:16). This adds to the perplexity in the Bible because if Jesus looked like someone else, then inevitably the person on the cross was someone made to appear to be Jesus, since Jesus was made to appear as someone else. This makes perfect sense in the Quran; otherwise, there would be no logical explanation for Jesus to be formed like someone else in the cave. (Continued from 120-140)

140. Jesus Heard?

Errancy; Are prayers answered according to the Bible, namely with one of the most righteous Prophets; Jesus?

The humble will be answered;

"If My people who are called by My name will humble themselves, and pray and seek My face, and turn from their wicked ways, then I will hear from heaven, and will forgive their sin and heal their land." (2 Chronicles 7:14)

The earnest and pure will be answered;

"If you would earnestly seek God and make your supplication to the Almighty, if you were pure and upright, surely now He would awake for you, and prosper your rightful habitation." (Job 8:5-6)

The fearful will be answered;

"He will fulfill the desire of them that fear him: he also will hear their cry, and will save them." (Psalms 145:19)

The righteous will be answered;

"The Lord is far from the wicked: but he hears the prayer of the righteous." (Proverbs 15:29)

Even Jesus himself teaches prayers will be answered; Prayers will be publicly answered;

"But you, when you pray, go into your room, and when you have shut your door, pray to your Father who is in the secret place; and your Father who sees in secret will reward you openly." (Matthew 6:6)

Everyone's prayers will be answered;

"Ask and it will be given to you; seek and you will find; knock and the door will be opened to you. For everyone who asks receives; he who seeks finds; and to him who knocks, the door will be opened." (Matthew 7:7-8)

If two pray together (i.e. Jesus and Mary or the Trinity), their prayers will be answered;

"if two of you on earth agree to ask anything at all, it will be granted to you by my Father in heaven." (Matthew 18:19)

The believers will be answered;

"If you believe, you will receive whatever you ask for in prayer." (Matthew 21:22)

Worshippers will be answered;

"The Lord said, "Now we know that God does not hear sinners; but if anyone is a worshiper of God and does His will, He hears him." (John 9:31)

We see that in general the righteous will be granted redemption upon request. Based on these prerequisites, the actions and words of Jesus amply qualify him for rescue.

We then see Jesus did indeed attempt to collect his due by praying for God to extricate him;

"And going a little farther he fell on his face and prayed, "My Father, if it be possible, let this cup pass from me; nevertheless, not as I will, but as thou wilt." (Matthew 26:39), (Mark 14:36), and (Luke 22:42)

Here, Jesus facing execution, prays to God for freedom, yet contrary to all the promises that the righteous will be saved; Jesus' desperate prayer is forsaken;

"With a loud cry Jesus died." (Mark 15:37) and (Matthew 27:50)

Here Jesus cries a second time, with no words recorded, and dies, while in Luke and John, contrary words were reported, yet the outcome was the same, death.

"Jesus cried out in a loud voice, "Father! In your hands I place my spirit!" He said this and died." (Luke 23:46) Or "Jesus drank the wine and said, "It is finished!" Then he bowed his head and gave up his spirit." (John 19:30)

In three of the four, Jesus cried at least once and prayed to be saved. In two of the four, Jesus cried a second time. In all four Gospels, Jesus appeared to have died, displaying neglect on the part of God in regards to the prayers of Jesus.

Adding insult to injury, because of this apparent unanswered prayer in the Bible, Jesus is portrayed as a disbelieving, doubtful, anxious man, wishing to be rescued, then lashing out when rejected;

"And about the ninth hour Jesus cried with a loud voice, "Eli, Eli, la'ma sabach-tha'ni?" that is, "My God, my God, why hast thou forsaken me?"" (Matthew 27:46)

Non-Christian religions see this unanswered prayer as a disqualification of Jesus, meaning, he did not fit the criteria to be saved, while the Quran teaches the Prayer of Jesus was answered.

Excuse; God wanted Jesus to die, that is why the prayers of Jesus to be saved were not answered.

Rebuttal: What? Here is where Christian apologetics confuse the Bible even more. On the one hand Christians claim Jesus is God, and as we have read, Jesus obviously wanted to be saved, therefore the triune god wanted to be saved from the cross. However, in order to explain the contradiction, the Christians try to have it both ways by saying at that moment, Jesus was not God, and the Real God did not want Jesus saved. They try to have their cake (sacrifice) and eat it too (salvation). Christians claim that their trinity is One God, if so, how could their 'One God' want two different things at that same moment? Here we uncover their fallacy because you cannot have One God fighting Himself to live.

Correction: Allah, being the Ultimate Authority, has issued a verdict settling the crucifixion incident;

"That they said (in boast), "We killed Christ Jesus the son of Mary, the Messenger of Allah"; - but they killed him not, nor crucified him, but so it was made to appear to them, and those who differ therein are full of doubts, with no (certain) knowledge, but only conjecture to follow, for of a surety they killed him not" (Quran 4:157)

Therefore, the Quran proves what Bible editors have been trying to hide, based on the differing testimonies from Mark, Matthew, Luke, and John, we the lawful jury find the defendants not guilty.

If the Christians love Jesus as much as they claim, the Christians would not insist Jesus was killed with all the conflicting evidence surrounding the murder, especially since he was found alive a few days later.

141. Turn cheek

Errancy; Jesus said, "do not defend yourselves" (Matthew 5:39, Matthew 26:52) *Vs* Jesus said, "defend yourselves" (Luke 22:36)

Excuse; Some Biblical words are being taken literally instead of symbolically or metaphorically. "turn the other cheek." Figuratively meant, "be moral".

Rebuttal: Actually, turn the other cheek was a literal commandment because Jesus himself demonstrated this law;

"When he had said this, one of the officers standing by struck Jesus with his hand, saying, "Is that how you answer the high priest?" Jesus answered him, "If I have spoken wrongly, bear witness to the wrong; but if I have spoken rightly, why do you strike me?" (John 18:22-23)

Rather than attacking the officer or causing the officer to evaporate (since Christians claim Jesus is God), instead Jesus reasons with the guard.

This means that if your enemy strikes or attacks you, you are to allow him or her to attack you without striking back. You are to take the punishment without reacting. If the Christians in history allowed themselves to be attacked without retaliating as Jesus ordered, than there would be no Christians left today.

Correction: The Quran saves the Bible regarding the rule given by Jesus by clarifying that when you are being attacked, it is best to have patience and forgiveness against the attack, But then if the attacks continue, than we are given the permission to retaliate only with the equal amount of force that was used against us:

"And if you take your turn, then retaliate with the like of that with which you were afflicted; But if ye endure patiently, verily it is better for the patient." (Quran 16:126)

Therefore, we are given the permission to repel attacks, to protect ourselves, although God prefers forgiveness.

142. son of man or Mary?

Errancy; In the Bible, Jesus is labeled "son of man" 85 times. It is logical to say that the scribes changed the word (Mary) into (man). With women having such a low status through out the Bible, it is likely that the Bible editors referred to Jesus as son of a "man" rather than son of a "woman". The Greek word for woman in the Bible is "oudemia" while the word for man cuts out the (mia). So we can see how the word woman could have, and is, cut to man.

If the Bible were free of alterations and changes, then it would have properly called Jesus "son of Mary", because like Adam, Jesus has no father, so it is simply illogical to call Jesus a son of man. Were the Bible writers ashamed to label Christ's origin from a woman?

Excuse; None available.

Correction: Because we are considered equal in the Quran and male pride or ego had no part in the creation of the Quran, Jesus was and is correctly named as "son of Mary" while the Bible still labels him as son of "man".

What ever their political or personal motivations, they are absent from the Quran, thank God;

"Behold! the angels said: "O Mary! Allah giveth thee glad tidings of a Word from Him: his name will be Messiah, Jesus, the son of Mary, held in honor in this world and the Hereafter and of (the company of) those nearest to Allah;" (Quran 3:45)

143. <u>Mary a Virgin or Young woman?</u>

Errancy; Jews and Christians argue among themselves regarding the use of (Isaiah 7:14) as a confirmation to the birth of Jesus;

"Therefore the Lord Himself will give you a sign: Behold, a virgin will be with child and bear a son, and she will call His name Immanuel," (Isaiah 7:14).

Yet Hebrew scholars attest that this passage is speaking of a maiden, not a virgin, thus concluding this not a prophecy.

The problem is dealing with the Hebrew word for virgin, which is "almah". According to the *Strong's Concordance* it means, "virgin, young woman 1a) of marriageable age 1b) maid or newly married." Therefore, the word "almah" does not always mean virgin. Additionally, there is a more accurate Hebrew word for virgin: "bethulah".

Excuse; Both have valid arguments against each other.

Rebuttal: In the days of Jesus, adultery laws were extremely strict, even deadly. Therefore, unless the maiden was identified as a married woman, then 99% of the time, she was a virgin.

Note; she was not called a harlot or adulterous as unmarried promiscuous women were labeled in the Bible, further proving she is a virgin as the majority of young women were during the days of Jesus.

Correction: The Quran crystallizes the fact that Mary was a virgin:

"And Mary the daughter of 'Imran, who guarded her chastity; and We breathed into (her body) of Our spirit; and she testified to the truth of the words of her Lord and of His Revelations, and was one of the devout (servants)." (Quran 66:12)

144. Filled with the Spirit?

Errancy; Jesus was filled with the Holy Spirit after death (John 7:39) *Vs* Jesus was filled with the Holy Spirit before birth (Luke 1:41, 67)

Excuse; None available.

Correction: Quran teaches Jesus had spirit all along and his mission was to teach, not be killed

"O People of the Book! Commit no excesses in your religion: Nor say of Allah aught but the truth. Christ Jesus the son of Mary was (no more than) a messenger of Allah, and His Word, which He bestowed on Mary, and a spirit proceeding from Him…" (Quran 4:171)

145. Jesus Judges?

Errancy; Jesus judges (John 5:22, 27, 9:39) *Vs* Jesus does not judge (John 3:17, 8:15, 12:47)

Excuse; Jesus the man does not Judge, but Jesus who will return in his second coming will judge.

Rebuttal: When the Bible claimed Jesus judges, it does not specify "during the second coming", thus, the contradiction remains.

Correction: The Quran teaches that Ultimate Judgment belongs to God alone, not Jesus:

"And if there is a party of you which believeth in that wherewith I have been sent, and there is a party which believeth not, then have patience until Allah judge between us. He is the Best of all who deal in judgment." (Quran 7:87)

"And (O Muhammad) follow that which is inspired in thee, and forbear until Allah give judgment. And He is the Best of Judges." (Quran 10:109)

146. <u>Jesus Demonized?</u>

Errancy; In an apparent oversight within the Bible, Jesus professes to be Lucifer, a serious flaw absent from the Quran.

Jesus and Satan in the Bible both have the same name; "Morning Star"

"King of Babylon, bright morning star, you have fallen from heaven! In the past you conquered nations, but now you have been thrown to the ground." (Isaiah 14:12)

Even the *KJV OT Hebrew Lexicon* states "morning star" means; Lucifer, light-bearer, king of Babylon and Satan.

Shockingly, Jesus then attributes this title to himself;

"I, Jesus, have sent my angel to give witness to you of these things in the churches. I am the root and the offspring of David, the bright and morning star." (Revelation 22:16)

Christians often use this method of self-ascription by Jesus in attempts to prove Jesus' divinity, for example;

"God said to Moses, "I am who I am". This is what you are to say to the Israelites: `I am' has sent me to you.'" (Exodus 3:14)

These Christians then link Exodus to try to explain that Jesus is God;

"I tell you the truth," Jesus answered, "Before Abraham was born, I am!" (John 8:58)

By the same Christian logic of transferring descriptive analogies from one Character in the Bible to another, Jesus is also personified as Satan.

Excuse; Mistranslation.

Rebuttal: (See Reply letter [I] in Rebuttal Chart)

Correction: In conclusion, while the Bible mistakenly demonizes Jesus, while the Quran calls Jesus: "The statement of the truth" (Quran 19:34), "Servant of God" (Quran 19:31) "The Messiah (Quran 9:31), and "with the spirit from God" (Quran 4:171).

147. <u>Did Jesus lie?</u>

Errancy; According to the Bible, Jesus is recorded as committing a lie;

"(Jesus said) "Go to the festival yourselves. I am not going to this festival, for my time has not yet fully come." After saying this, he remained in Galilee; but after his brothers had gone to the festival, he went also, not openly, but in secret." (John 7:8-10)

Excuse; it was not a lie because Jesus did not go in the fashion the brothers wanted him to, they wanted Jesus to go openly and Jesus went privately.

Rebuttal: The issue is not the walking technique of Jesus, the subject is that Jesus stated, "I'm not going", and as soon as the brothers left, Jesus broke his word and went.

Correction: The Quran does not confirm that such a lie occurred, instead the Quran states that Jesus is the word of God, hence the Truth and a statement of Truth:

"Behold! the angels said: "O Mary! Allah giveth thee glad tidings of a Word from Him: his name will be Christ Jesus, the son of Mary, held in honor in this world and the Hereafter and of (the company of) those nearest to Allah" (Quran 3:45)

"Such (was) Jesus the son of Mary: (it is) a statement of truth, about which they (vainly) dispute." (Quran 19:34)

148. Witness True?

Errancy; The testimony of Jesus was true (John 8:14) *Vs* The testimony of Jesus was false (John 5:31)

Excuse; All men are liars, thus Jesus the man was a false witness before the Jews, but Jesus the God was a true witness.

Rebuttal: Here the apologetics give us more confusion. A liar cannot be an honest man. And an honest man is not a liar. Yes, an honest man can lie but it would be degrading to call God a liar or –false witness-.

Correction: The Holy Quran explains that Jesus was not God but that his witness is True. Jesus is assigned by God in the Quran to be a witness and never states that Christ's witness is false:

"And there is none of the People of the Book but must believe in him before his death; and on the Day of Judgment he will be a witness against them;" (Quran 4:159)

149. Sent to World?

Errancy; Do not preach to the Samaritans (Matthew 10:5-6) *Vs* Preach to the Samaritans (John 4:4-41, Acts 8:5, 14, 15, 25)

Excuse; both are correct; at first Jesus came for Jews only, after the Jews rejected Jesus, and the assumed resurrection, they were to preach to the Gentiles as Paul explains;

"to the Jew first, and also to the Greek" (Romans 1:16)

Rebuttal: There are multi-problems with this excuse;

First, why not go to the gentiles from the start, especially when Jesus spent 10 years in Egypt (Matthew 2:13-23).

Second, Christians claim Jesus is God, and the Bible says that God does not change His mind (1 Samuel 15:29); Therefore Jesus cannot go from cursing gentiles to saving them.

Third, When Jesus was presumably resurrected, he could have traveled around the world preaching, instead he stayed in –Israel-.

Forth, after the resurrection and even after Jesus left the earth, the disciples were still instructed not to preach to gentiles (Acts 11:2-3)

Correction: The Quran clarifies that Jesus was only sent to the children of Israel:

"And remember, Jesus, the son of Mary, said: "O Children of Israel! I am the messenger of Allah (sent) to you, confirming the Law (which came) before me, and giving Glad Tidings of a Messenger to come after me, whose name shall be Ahmad." But when he came to them with Clear Signs, they said, "this is evident sorcery!" (Quran 61:6)

"And behold! I did restrain the Children of Israel from (violence to) thee when thou didst show them the clear Signs, and the unbelievers among them said: 'This is nothing but evident magic.'" (Quran 5:110)

150. Shepherd or Sheep?

Errancy; Jesus is a Shepherd (John 10:11) *Vs* Jesus is a sheep (John 1:29)

Excuse; Jesus was both; guided people to accept his sacrifice.

Rebuttal: if he came to teach (Shepherd), he would have taught for the rest of his natural life, if he came to be a sacrifice (sheep), he would have allowed himself to be caught and killed when he was being chased at childhood (Matthew 2:14) because a sacrificial lamb is only valid as a child;

"You may choose either a sheep or a goat, but it must be a one-year-old male" (Exodus 12:5)

Correction: The Quran tells us that Jesus came as a Shepherd (teacher and Prophet) with the intentions of giving wisdom, not shedding blood:

"When Jesus came with clear proofs (of Allah's Sovereignty), he said: I have come unto you with wisdom, and to make plain some of that concerning which ye differ. So keep your duty to Allah, and obey me." (Quran 43:63)

151. Christ Cursed?

Errancy; Jesus is cursed (Galatians 3:13) *Vs* Jesus is not cursed (Psalms 72:17)

Excuse; Jesus was both; cursed on earth and blessed in Heaven.

Rebuttal: the apologetics are willing to stoop to new depths to avoid a disparity. It's shocking that they're willing to call their presumed God and savior "Cursed" while the Bible says it's Satan who's the cursed one (Genesis 3:14).

Correction: The Quran corrects the Biblical insult on Prophet Jesus by saying Jesus was blessed on earth and the Afterlife:

"Behold! the angels said: "O Mary! Allah giveth thee glad tidings of a Word from Him: his name will be Christ Jesus, the son of Mary, held in honor in this world and the Hereafter and of (the company of) those nearest to Allah" (Quran 3:45)

152. Descended to Hell?

Errancy; Jesus descended to Hell;

"For Christ also hath once suffered for sins, the just for the unjust, that he might bring us to God, being put to death in the flesh, but quickened by the Spirit: By which also he went and preached unto the spirits in prison; Which sometime were disobedient, when once the longsuffering of God waited in the days of Noah, while the ark was a preparing, wherein few, that is, eight souls were saved by water." (1 Peter 3:18–20)

Note; (1 Peter 3:18–20) is reiterated in the (Apostles' Creed) as "[Jesus] who was conceived of the Holy Spirit, born of the Virgin Mary, suffered under Pontius Pilate, was crucified, died, buried and descended into hell."

Vs

Jesus ascended to Heaven (Luke 23:43)

Excuse; the doomed in (1 Peter 3:18 – 20) were angels in Heaven that Jesus tried to save; therefore Jesus went to Heaven, not Hell.

Rebuttal: To claim Jesus was trying to save angels to avoid the embarrassing Biblical claim that Jesus descended to Hell rather than Heaven, is an affront to the obvious Bible passages and creed that say otherwise. Selective reading will not grant escape from Jesus descending to Hell in the Bible.

First, the reason why the unsaved souls in (1 Peter 3:18–20) were not angels is because they were from "days of Noah, while the ark was being prepared". We know that angels were created before men (Job 38:4-7).

Second, we know Jesus was not rescuing unsaved angels in Heaven because according to the Bible; Heaven is a place for the righteous while the abode for unsaved angels is "Hell" (Matthew 25:41).

In (2 Peter 2:4), the imprisoned angels are in "Tartarus", a Greek word used to describe a place 'Lower than Hell'. Therefore, in an effort to defend Jesus from being in Hell, they have exposed Jesus to be in "Tartarus", a place lower than Hell.

Note; Some Christians try to insinuate that the Holy Quran suggests that Jesus will go to Hell because those who worship idols and their idols will go to Hell (Quran 21:98). The Jesus in the Gospel is similar yet different from the Jesus in the Quran in that there is no ambiguity concerning the entity of Jesus. The Islamic Jesus will not go to Hell, because Muslims do not worship the Quranic Jesus. The idols referenced in the Holy Quran may be the crosses and statues sprawled across most Churches.

Correction: The Quran corrects the Biblical insult on Prophet Jesus by saying Jesus went to Heaven, not Hell:

"Nay, Allah raised him up unto Himself; and Allah is Exalted in Power, Wise" (Quran 4:158)

153. **First to be Resurrected?**

Errancy; Jesus was the first to be resurrected (1 Corinthians 15:20) *Vs* Others were resurrected before Jesus (1 Kings 17:22; 2 Kings 13:21)

Excuse; others were a resuscitation while Jesus was a resurrection because Jesus was immortal.

Rebuttal: In an effort to correct a discrepancy, the Biblicists add more contradictions. First, if Jesus were genuinely immortal, then he would not have died in the first place.

Second, the Bible uses the word "resurrected", not "resuscitated" as the apologetics would prefer.

Correction: The Quran corrects the Bible in that it indicates that there have been resurrections before Jesus and never states that Jesus was the only to be resurrected:

"Or (take) the similitude of one who passed by a hamlet, all in ruins to its roofs. He said: "Oh! how shall Allah bring it (ever) to life, after (this) its death?" but Allah caused him to die for a hundred years, then raised him up (again). He said: "How long didst thou tarry (thus)?" He said: (Perhaps) a day or part of a day." He said: "Nay, thou hast tarried thus a hundred years; but look at thy food and thy drink; they show no signs of age; and look at thy donkey: And that We may make of thee a sign unto the people, Look further at the bones, how We bring them together and clothe them with flesh." When this was shown clearly to him, he said: "I know that Allah hath power over all things." (Quran 2:259)

154. **First Born?**

Errancy; "(Jesus) who is the image of the invisible God, the firstborn of every creature" (Colossians 1:15) *Vs* "By him (Jesus) all things were created: things in heaven and on earth, visible and invisible, whether thrones or powers or rulers or authorities." (Colossians 1:16)

There is confusion as to when Jesus was created (either first, as was Adam) or (centuries later through Mary). One thing is clear, that is Jesus was created, and by definition, not the Creator.

Excuse; Mistranslation of the Greek word "prototokos" which should read "pre-eminent" instead of "first born"; making Jesus the creator rather than the created.

Rebuttal: (See Reply letter [I] in Rebuttal Chart).

Correction: The Quran teaches that Adam was the first-born and that Jesus was made in a similar fashion to Adam's creation:

"It is He Who has created you from a single person (Adam), and (then) He has created from him his wife (Eve), in order that he might enjoy the pleasure of living with her. ..." (Quran 7:189)

"The similitude of Jesus before Allah is as that of Adam; He created him from dust, then said to him: "Be". And he was." (Quran 3:59)

155. <u>Mary a Sinner?</u>

Errancy; Protestants argue against Catholics regarding the status of Mary. Protestants argue she was a sinner (Luke 1:46) *Vs* Catholics argue Mary was sinless (Luke 1:28)

Excuse; Both have valid arguments against each other.

Correction: The Holy Quran corrects multiple misconceptions concerning the mother of the Messiah. The Quran confirms that Mary was made pure, so she was in a state of imperfection and later made pure:

"Behold! the angels said: "O Mary! Allah hath chosen thee and purified thee- chosen thee above the women of all nations." (Quran 3:42)

156. <u>Hypocrite?</u>

Errancy; The Bible insults Jesus by portraying him as a hypocrite. Jesus in the Bible says; 'Anyone who calls another a fool is liable to Hell'. (Matthew 5:22) while shortly afterwards, Jesus says that anyone who hears his words and does not do them is a fool. (Matthew 7:26)

Moving forward, (Matthew 23:17-19) Jesus twice calls the Pharisees blind fools. (Matthew 25:2-3, 8) Jesus compares the maidens who took no oil to fools. Thus, Jesus hypocritically commits the same sin he preached against in the Bible.

Excuse; That is what it says but that is not what it means

Rebuttal: (See Reply letter [E] in Rebuttal Chart) The word "fool" has no dual meaning. Whether the phrase is said angrily or softly, (which Jesus said in both tones), the word still has the same meaning.

Correction: God clears Jesus of hypocrisy in the Holy Quran. The Quran clarifies that Jesus was upright, honorable, and spoke the Good News from Allah, not profanity:

"I have come unto you with wisdom, and to make plain some of that concerning which ye differ. So keep your duty to Allah, and obey me." (Quran 43:63)

"Then We caused Our messengers to follow in their footsteps; and We caused Jesus, son of Mary, to follow, and gave him the Gospel, and placed compassion and mercy in the hearts of those who followed him. But monasticism they invented. We ordained it not for them. Only seeking Allah's pleasure, and they observed it not with right observance. So We give those of them who believe their reward, but many of them are evil livers." (Quran 57:27)

"O ye who believe! Be Allah's helpers, even as Jesus son of Mary said unto the disciples: Who are my helpers for Allah? They said: We are Allah's helpers. And a party of the Children of Israel believed, while a party disbelieved. Then We strengthened those who believed against their foe, and they became the uppermost." (Quran 61:14)

157. Forgiveness before Jesus?

Errancy; People before Jesus went to Heaven (2 Kings 2:11) *Vs* No one will go to Heaven unless they accept Jesus (John 10:9, 14:6).

Excuse; The Bible confirms that previous prophets believed in God (James 2:23), which is the same as believing in Jesus.

Rebuttal: According to Paul, believing in Jesus was not enough; one had to accept the supposed blood sacrifice of Jesus (Romans 5:9) which was impossible for previous people to postulate because Jesus had not yet come to earth.

Correction: The Holy Quran displays a fair system of salvation, which gives accountability to past and future creations of God.

"... No laden soul will bear another's load." (Quran 39:7)

And

"Surely Allah does not do injustice to the weight of an atom, and if it is a good deed He multiplies it and gives from Himself a great reward." (Quran 4:40)

158. Said Everything?

Errancy; Jesus said everything to his disciples (John 15:15) *Vs* Jesus did not say everything to his disciples (John 16:12)

Excuse; That is what it says but that is not what it means. (John 15:15) is speaking of present tense, not future tense.

Rebuttal: (See Reply letter [E] in Rebuttal Chart). The problem is that these Bible followers believe that Jesus himself is God, so from the Christian perspective, (John 15:15) is saying "Everything I know from myself I let you know". This remains a direct contradiction with (John 16:12) which states there is still much more they will be told. The question arises; did God learn something new from one chapter to the next?

Correction: The Quran corrects and confirms that Jesus was being honest when he said, "there was much more to be told by someone else".

"Those who follow the messenger, the unlettered Prophet, whom they find mentioned in their own (scriptures), - in the law and the Gospel; - for he commands them what is just and forbids them what is evil; he allows them as lawful what is good (and pure) and prohibits them from what is bad (and impure); He releases them from their heavy burdens and from the yokes that are upon them. So it is those who believe in him, honor him, help him, and follow the light which is sent down with him, - it is they who will prosper". (Quran 7:157)

159. Abolished the Laws?

Errancy; Jesus did not come to abolish the law. (Matthew 5:17-19, Luke 16:17) *Vs* Jesus did abolish the law. (Ephesians 2:13-15, Hebrews 7:18-19)

Excuse; The laws were supposed to be followed until the resurrection, after the resurrection, the laws were done away with;

"Purge out therefore the old leaven, that ye may be a new lump, as ye are unleavened. For even Christ our Passover is sacrificed for us" (1 Corinthians 5:7)

Rebuttal: It is a faulty notion to claim the laws, which were followed for millenniums, were only made to be temporary. Both the God of Abraham and Jesus state the laws are forever;

"Everlasting" ,"For All Generations", "a Perpetual Ordinance " (Exodus 27:21; 28:43; 29:28; 30:21; 31:17; Leviticus 6:18, 22; 7:34, 36; 10:9, 15; 17:7; 23:14, 21, 41; 24:3; Numbers 10:8; 15:15; 18:8, 11, 19, 23; 19:10; Deuteronomy 5:29; Psalms 119:160) and is not to be changed or taken away from (Deuteronomy 4:2; 12:32).

Jesus confirms the Laws are for all generations and everlasting by following the laws (Matthew 8:4, 26:19, John 7:10).

Actions speak louder than words and besides the actions of Jesus keeping the Everlasting Laws, Jesus also states;

"Think not that I am come to destroy the law, or the prophets: I am not come to destroy, but to fulfill. For verily I say unto you, Till heaven and earth pass, one jot or one title shall in no wise pass from the law, till all be fulfilled." (Matthew 5:17-18)

In conclusion, the God of Abraham in the Bible, the Prophets, and the Messiah all say the Laws are unending. The Righteous have one Enemy, he who leads people astray by through lethargy.

Correction: God through the Holy Quran explains that it is a combination of Faith and Works that gives us Salvation:

"For Him (alone) is prayer in Truth: any others that they call upon besides Him hear them no more than if they were to stretch forth their hands for water to reach their mouths but it reaches them not: for the prayer of those without Faith is nothing but (futile) wandering (in the mind)." (Quran 13:14)

The Holy Quran explains that works are to our benefit:

"O you whose hearts have been touched with the divine hand: When you intend to stand before God for performing your act of worship, then ablution becomes a duty. Wash your faces, your hands and the forearms up to the elbows, and with your wet hands wipe your heads, then wash your feet to the ankles....God does not intend to put you in difficulty but only to make you sound headed men of proper discipline and excellent mind, and to set you upon a course of purity of thought and action, for the actions of men are best interpreters of their thoughts, and He means to make all grace abound in you that you may hopefully actuate yourselves with the feeling of gratitude and gratefulness and lift Him your inward sight." (Quran 5:6)

The Holy Quran teaches us that Jesus came only to clarify the previous scripture, not to change it, and to promote the most important law, to worship our Creator:

"When Jesus came with clear proofs (of Allah's Sovereignty), he said: I have come unto you with wisdom, and to make plain some of that concerning which ye differ. So keep your duty to Allah, and obey me."

"For Allah, He is my Lord and your Lord: so worship ye Him: this is a Straight Way." (Quran 43:63-64)

(VIII.) TRINITY

160. <u>King of All?</u>

Errancy; There is a multidimensional problem in the Bible with the claim that Jesus is the King of kings. First, within his lifetime, Jesus never claimed to be the King of Kings, only the King of Jews;

[King of Jews] "Then Pilate asked Him, "Are You the King of the Jews?" He answered and said to him, "It is as you say." (Mark 15:2)

Second, briefly after Jesus claimed to be the King of Jews, he was disproved;

[Invalidated King] "Let the Christ, the King of Israel, descend now from the cross that we may see and believe." Even those who were crucified with Him reviled Him." (Mark 15:32)

Third, after the passing of Jesus, Paul in an attempt to deify him says;

[King of all] "The Lamb will overcome them because he is the Lord of Lords and King of kings" (Revelation 17:14)

The Problem with Paul calling Jesus the King of all is three fold, 1) Jesus never claimed to be the King of all, only of Jews. 2) Jesus supposedly died on the cross, discrediting his Kingship. 3) the title "King of Kings" is already taken by another man;

"Artaxerxes, King of Kings, To Ezra the priest, a scribe of the Law of the God of heaven: Perfect peace, and so forth." (Ezra 7:12)

Therefore, the title "King of Kings" regarding Jesus in the Bible is not only unclaimed and discredited by Jesus, but also conflicts with other "men" who bore the title.

Excuse; None available.

Correction: In the Holy Quran, no other living creature as in the Bible [(Ezekiel 26:7), (1 Kings 10:23), (Ezra 7:12) and (Revelation 17:14)], has been called "King of Kings except for God alone:

"High above all is Allah, the King, the Truth! Be not in haste with the Quran before its revelation to thee is completed, but say, "O my Lord! advance me in knowledge." (Quran 20:114)

And

"All that is in the heavens and all that is in the earth glorifieth Allah, the King, the Holy, the Mighty, the Wise." (Quran 62:1)

And

"He is Allah, besides Whom there is no god; the King, the Holy, the Giver of peace, the Granter of security, Guardian over all, the Mighty, the Supreme, the Possessor of every greatness Glory be to Allah from what they set up (with Him)." (Quran 59:23) (Continued from 160 to 189)

161. The Holy One?

Errancy; "We believe and know that you are the Holy One of God. (John 6:69) *Vs* "And Jesus said to him, "Why do you call me good? No one is good but God alone." (Mark 10:18)

Excuse; That is what it says but that is not what it means. Astoundingly, apologetics reinterpret (Mark 10:18) to say; 'do you realize your calling me God'

Rebuttal: (See Reply letter [E] in Rebuttal Chart). The Bible scholars ignore the context yet the preceding passage debunks their distortion;

"a man ran up and knelt before him, and asked him, good teacher" (Mark 10:17)

Therefore, Jesus was being called a teacher, as were other men including Barnabas and Simeon (Acts 13:1)

In fact, according to Paul, a "teacher" is fourth in the chain of authority;

"And God hath set some in the church, first apostles, secondarily prophets, thirdly teachers, after that miracles, then gifts of healings, helps, governments, diversities of tongues." (1 Corinthians 12:28)

The first is God, second are the apostles (obviously Paul thinks highly of himself), and third in line of religiousness are the Prophets, and Fourth are the Teachers. Therefore, it is a far stretch for the Bible scholars to take the word "teacher" in (Mark 10:17) and make it jump to the head of the Spiritual line.

Thus, the man approaching Jesus had no objective of calling Jesus "divine"; instead, the man was simply complimenting Jesus as "smart".

A "good teacher" is smart, informed, and knowledgeable. At this point, Jesus refuted the man saying, "Only God is good", meaning; only God has all the knowledge, above all others in wisdom. We understand this meaning as it is repeated by Jesus in this passages;

"But of that day and hour no one knows, not even the angels in heaven, nor the Son, but only the Father." (Mark 13:32)

And

"So Jesus answered them, "My teaching is not mine, but His who sent me" (John 7:16)

The second reason we know the word "teacher" in (Mark 10:17) has no Divine significance is because throughout the entire Bible, God is never referred to with the noun: "Teacher".

In conclusion, for Christians to warp a passage where Jesus is clearly denying being the Holy One (and does not deny being a "teacher" – the fourth in line of religious stature-), is a disservice to humanity.

Correction: "Allah is He, than Whom there is no other god;- the Sovereign, the Holy One, the Source of Peace (and Perfection), the Guardian of Faith, the Preserver of Safety, the Exalted in Might, the Irresistible, the Supreme: Glory to Allah! (High is He) above the partners they attribute to Him." (Quran 59:23) (Continued from 160 to 189)

162. The Peace?

Errancy; "God was pleased through him to reconcile to himself all things by making peace through his blood, shed on the cross." (Colossians 1:19, 20) *Vs* "Think not that I am come to send peace on earth: I came not to send peace, but a sword." (Matthew 10:34)

Excuse; that is what it says but that is not what it means; there is a distinction between the purpose and the result.

Rebuttal: (See Reply letter [E] in Rebuttal Chart); We still see that even if we only focus on the result (rather than the purpose to "send a sword to earth"); Jesus came and left us with commotion since his birth.

"He gave orders to kill all the boys in Bethlehem and its neighborhood who were two years old and younger-this was done in accordance with what he had learned from the visitors about the time when the star had appeared." (Matthew 2:16)

And after Jesus departed;

"Then some Jews came from Antioch and Iconium and won the crowd over. They stoned Paul and dragged him outside the city, thinking he was dead." (Acts 14:19)

We see that when Jesus came to the earth and when he departed from the earth, there was commotion as was the case with all Prophets and no peace, even to this day, wars continue. The farfetched claim that Jesus reconciled "all things" by "making peace through his blood" possesses any validity. "All things" were and are not at peace as the Bible claims Jesus established.

Correction: The Holy Quran clarifies that God, unlike Jesus, can truly bring peace but that peace is conditional on the humans' freedom to choose peace. If humans seek love, they will receive love, so the Quran gives us multiple corrections in that 1) there was no unconditional blood sacrifice in the Quran and 2) God teaches how to Truly attain Peace in the Quran:

"And remember Abraham said: "My Lord, make this a City of Peace, and feed its people with fruits,-such of them as believe in Allah and the Last Day." He answered: As for him who disbelieveth, I shall leave him in contentment for a while, then I shall compel him to the doom of Fire - a hapless journey's end!" (Quran 2:126)

Therefore, God answered the prayer of Prophet Abraham, but specified the conditions for peace.

"Wherewith Allah guideth him who seeks His good pleasure to ways of peace and safety, and leadeth them out of darkness, by His will, unto the light,- guideth them to a path that is straight." (Quran 5:16)

Peace is not granted unconditionally to everyone through a blood sacrifice as the Bible claims; instead, there are various realistic conditions to receive Peace from the Giver of Peace:

"But if the enemy inclines towards peace, do thou (also) incline towards peace, and trust in Allah: for He is One that heareth and knoweth (all things)." (Quran 8:61)

Other than the conditions for peace on earth, the Quran clarifies that the ultimate place of Peace is in Heaven, where tranquility is truly conciliated:

"(This will be) their cry therein: "Glory to Thee, O Allah!" And "Peace" will be their greeting therein! and the close of their cry will be: "Praise be to Allah, the Cherisher and Sustainer of the worlds!" (Quran 10:10)

"But Allah doth call to the Home of Peace: He doth guide whom He pleaseth to a way that is straight." (Quran 10:25)

In conclusion, God teaches us 1) peace on earth is conditional 2) those who sincerely seek peace will receive peace; 3) the ultimate place of peace is Heaven. Finally, unlike Jesus, God in the Quran is the Source of Peace:

"Allah is He, than Whom there is no other god;- the Sovereign, the Holy One, the Source of Peace (and Perfection), the Guardian of Faith, the Preserver of Safety, the Exalted in Might, the Irresistible, the Supreme: Glory to Allah! (High is He) above the partners they attribute to Him. (Quran 59:23) (Continued from 160 to 189)

163. Trusted?

Errancy; "Trust in God; trust also in me (John 14:1) *Vs* "(Jesus said) "Go to the festival yourselves. I am not going to this festival, for my time has not yet fully come." After saying this, he remained in Galilee; but after his brothers had gone to the festival, he went also, not openly, but in secret." (John 7:8-10)

Excuse; It was not a lie because Jesus did not go in the fashion the brothers wanted him to, they wanted Jesus to go openly, and Jesus went privately.

Rebuttal: The issue is not whether Jesus was intending to go privately instead of out in the open, the subject is that Jesus claimed to have stated

"I'm not going", and as soon as the brothers left, In the Bible, Jesus is depicted to have broken his word and went.

Correction: We see from the Quran we can consistently put our Trust in God "And put thy trust in Him Who lives and dies not; and celebrate his praise; and enough is He to be acquainted with the faults of His servants" (Quran 25:58)

And

"(But) among (their) Allah-fearing men were two on whom Allah had bestowed His grace: They said: "Assault them at the (proper) Gate: when once ye are in, victory will be yours; But on Allah put your trust if ye have faith." (Quran 5:23)

And

"Our Lord can reach out to the utmost recesses of things by His knowledge. In the Allah is our trust. our Lord! decide Thou between us and our people in truth, for Thou art the best to decide." (Quran 7:89)

We see that Allah has and is Trusted while even as Jesus was allegedly on the cross, he was not trusted in (Mark 15:32) (Continued from 160 to 189)

164. The Protector?

Errancy; The Bible alleges that those who are one with Jesus will be protected by Jesus "I am the gate: whoever enters through me will be kept safe." (John 10:9)

Besides the fact that according to the Bible, Jesus did not even protect himself (irrespective of repeated efforts) on the cross – we also witness that the self proclaimed number one apostle of Jesus; [Paul] was also not kept safe, despite the alleged promise of safety from Jesus;

"Then some Jews came from Antioch and Iconium and won the crowd over. They stoned Paul and dragged him outside the city, thinking he was dead." (Acts 14:19)

Therefore, Jesus did not have the sole power to be a protector for himself or those devoted to him.

Excuse; God wanted Jesus to die, which is why the prayers by Jesus to protect himself were not answered.

Rebuttal: Here is where Christian apologetics confuse the Bible even more. On the one hand, Christians claim Jesus is God, and as we have read, Jesus obviously wanted to be saved; therefore, it would seem that triune god wanted to be protected from the cross.

Nevertheless, in order to explain the contradiction, the Christians try to have it both ways by saying at that moment, Jesus was not God, and the Real God did not want Jesus saved.

The Christians try to have their cake (sacrifice) and eat it too (salvation). Christians claim that their trinity is One God, if so, how could their 'One God' want two different things at that same moment? Here we uncover the fallacy because you cannot have One God fighting Himself to live.

Correction: The Holy Quran corrects this multi-mistake in the Bible by stating:

"Allah is the Protector of those who have faith: from the depths of darkness He will lead them forth into light. Of those who reject faith the patrons are the evil ones: from light they will lead them forth into the depths of darkness. They will be companions of the fire, to dwell. (Quran 2:257) and God's Protection Power extended to Jesus the moment Jesus asked to be protected (Quran 4:157) as the Protection of God in the Quran extended to Prophet Muhammad:

"Muhammad was sitting under a tree when a pagan with a sword approached him to kill him, the pagan asked 'who will protect you', Muhammad replied "Allah", at this moment, the pagan lunged forward at Prophet Muhammad tripped on a stump and dropped the sword which Muhammad picked up and gave it back to the pagan and asked the pagan, "who would have protected you", the pagan replied 'no, one', from that day on, the pagan became a Muslim and one of Prophet Muhammad's closest companions. (Volume 5, Book 59, Number 460: Narrated Jabir bin 'Abdullah) (Continued from 160 to 189)

165. Mighty and Powerful?

Errancy; "Christ, who is the head over every power and authority" (Colossians 2:10) *Vs* "I can of Myself do nothing. As I hear, I judge; and My judgment is righteous, because I do not seek My own will but the will of the Father who sent Me." (John 5:30)

Excuse; You must understand the context of the verse.

Rebuttal: (See Reply letter [C] in Rebuttal Chart). The context clearly goes on about how Jesus is defunct without his Creator.

Correction: "Have they not traveled in the land and seen the nature of the consequence for those who were before them, and they were mightier than these in power? Allah is not such that aught in the heavens or in the earth escapeth Him. Lo! He is the Wise, the Mighty." (Quran 35:44)

And

"To the People of Pharaoh, too, aforetime, came Warners (from Allah). The (people) rejected all Our Signs; Therefore We grasped them with the grasp of the Mighty, the Powerful." (Quran 54:41-42) (Continued from 160 to 189)

166. The Omnipotent One?

Errancy; "Christ died and returned to life so that he might be the Lord of both the living and the dead." (Romans 14:9) *Vs* "You heard me say, `I am going away and I am coming back to you.' If you loved me, you would be glad that I am going to the Father, for the Father is greater than I." (John 14:28)

Excuse; That is what it says but that is not what it means. The son is less than the Father in rank, but not in nature.

Rebuttal: (See Reply letter [E] in Rebuttal Chart). At least we got a partial confession from the Bible scholars that Jesus is less than God. In summary, if Jesus is less than his Creator in any fashion, form or function (as Jesus himself admits), then logically, Jesus is not equal to God. For example: one cannot have less work than their co-worker and also claim to have an equal amount. One can say they are doing the same work, but analytically one's work is greater than the other is. The president and vice president are not equal even though they act as one in the company.

Correction: "Surely those who guard (against evil) shall be in gardens and rivers, In an Assembly of Truth, in the Presence of a Sovereign Omnipotent." (Quran 54:54-55)

And

"He is the Omnipotent, (watching) from above over His worshippers, and He sets guardians over you. At length, when death approaches one of you, Our angels take his soul, and they never fail in their duty." (Quran 6:61) (Continued from 160 to 189)

167. The Creator?

Errancy; "By him (Jesus) all things were created: things in heaven and on earth, visible and invisible, whether thrones or powers or rulers or authorities." (Colossians 1:16) *Vs* "(Jesus) who is the image of the invisible God, the firstborn of every creature" (Colossians 1:15) *Vs* "And, behold, thou shalt conceive in thy womb, and bring forth a son, and shalt call his name Jesus." (Luke 1:31)

There is confusion as to when Jesus was created (either first, as was Adam) or (centuries later through Mary). One thing is clear, that is Jesus was created, and by definition, not the Creator.

Excuse; Mistranslation of the Greek word "prototokos" which should read "pre-eminent" instead of "first born"; making Jesus the creator rather than the created.

Rebuttal: (See Reply letter [I] in Rebuttal Chart). The Bible is riddled with translation errors. The translators can use anyone of the multi-meanings of vague words to insinuate deity to many of the characters in the Bible, including Jesus, the only problem with this insinuation is that it contradicts other parts of the Bible that disprove their divinity.

Correction: The Holy Quran which is kept authentic in its original language (Arabic) clarifies that Jesus was "created" like Adam (Quran 3:59) and that only God is the Creator:

"Those who celebrate the praises of Allah, standing, sitting, and reclining, and contemplate the (wonders of) creation in the heavens and the earth, (With the thought): "Our Lord! not for naught Hast Thou created (all) this! Glory to Thee! Give us salvation from the penalty of the Fire." (Quran 3:191) (Continued from 160 to 189)

168. The Forgiver?

Errancy; In one Gospel, there is the claim; "The Son of Man has authority on earth to forgive sins." (Mark 2:10) While in the Gospel of Luke, Jesus proves he has no authority to forgive;

164

"And Jesus said Father forgive them for they know not what they do." (Luke 23:34)

This passage demonstrates that Jesus himself did not have the unconstrained power to forgive. Jesus also confirms his lack of power;

"To sit at my right hand and at my left is not mine to grant, but it is for those for whom it has been prepared by my Father" (Matthew 20:23)

Correction: "Say: "If ye do love Allah, Follow me: Allah will love you and forgive you your sins: For Allah is Oft-Forgiving, Most Merciful." (Quran 3:31) (Continued from 160 to 189)

169. The Omniscient?

Errancy; "Christ, in whom are hidden all the treasures of wisdom an knowledge." (Colossians 2:3) *Vs* Jesus unaware of where the body of Lazarus is; "And [Jesus] said, Where have ye laid him? They said unto him, Lord, come and see." (John 11:34) and "But of that day and hour no one knows, not even the angels in heaven, nor the Son, but only the Father." (Mark 13:32)

Excuse; Due to Jesus being in 'flesh-man form', he did not know everything.

Rebuttal: Here we have another confession from the Bible scholars that Jesus was not equal to God, therefore discrediting trinity. In order to justify (Mark 13:32), they confirm the contradiction in (Colossians 2:3) that claims Jesus knows everything while Jesus himself acknowledged ignorance.

Correction: "Say: None in the heavens or on earth, except Allah, knows what is hidden: nor can they perceive when they shall be raised up (for Judgment)." (Quran 27:65)

And

"Say: "Allah knows best how long they stayed: with Him is (the knowledge of) the secrets of the heavens and the earth: how clearly He sees, how finely He hears (everything)! They have no protector other than Him; nor does He share His Command with any person whatsoever." (Quran 18:26) (Continued from 160 to 189)

170. The Most High?

Errancy; "God exalted him to the highest place and gave him a name that is above every name." (Philippians 2:9) *Vs* "(Now that he (Jesus) ascended, what is it but that he also descended first into the lower parts of the earth?" (Ephesians 4:9)

And

"For Christ also hath once suffered for sins, the just for the unjust, that he might bring us to God, being put to death in the flesh, but quickened by the Spirit: By which also he went and preached unto the spirits in prison; Which sometime were disobedient, when once the longsuffering of God waited in the days of Noah, while the ark was a preparing, wherein few, that is, eight souls were saved by water." (1 Peter 3:18 – 20)

Note; (1 Peter 3:18 – 20) is reiterated in the (Apostles' Creed) as "[Jesus] who was conceived of the Holy Spirit, born of the Virgin Mary, suffered under Pontius Pilate, was crucified, died, buried and descended into hell."

Excuse; 1st) Jesus went to Hell to try to save some of the doomed. 2nd) the doomed were angels in Heaven that Jesus tried to save.

Rebuttal: 1st) This confirms Jesus is not the highest because his abode was the lowest in the Bible. God in the Quran is always the Highest, Most Supreme. 2nd) To claim Jesus was trying to save angels to avoid the embarrassing Biblical claim that Jesus descended to Hell rather than Heaven, is an affront to the obvious Bible passages and creed that says otherwise. Selective reading will not grant escape from Jesus descending to Hell in the Bible.

First, the reason why the unsaved souls in (1 Peter 3:18 – 20) were not angels is because they were from "days of Noah, while the ark was being prepared". We know that angels were created before men (Job 38:4-7).

Second, we know Jesus was not rescuing unsaved angels in Heaven because according to the Bible; Heaven is a place for the righteous while the abode for unsaved angels is "Hell" (Matthew 25:41).

In (2 Peter 2:4), the imprisoned angels are in "Tartarus", a Greek word used to describe a place 'Lower than Hell'. Therefore, in an effort to defend Jesus from being in Hell, they have exposed Jesus to be in "Tartarus", a place lower than Hell.

Note; Some Christians try to insinuate that the Holy Quran suggests that Jesus will go to Hell because those who worship idols and their idols will go to Hell (Quran 21:98). The Jesus in the Gospel is similar yet different from the Jesus in the Quran in that there is no ambiguity concerning the entity of Jesus. Jesus will not go to Hell, because Muslims do not worship Jesus and Jesus never asked to be worshipped. The idols referenced in the Holy Quran may be the crosses and statues sprawled across most Churches.

Correction: Without dispute, the Holy Quran confirms God is the Highest: "His Throne doth extend over the heavens and the earth, and He feeleth no fatigue in guarding and preserving them for He is the Most High, the Supreme (in glory)." (Quran 2:255) (Continued from 160 to 189)

171. <u>The Appreciative?</u>

Errancy; "Behold, I am coming soon! My reward is with me and I will give to everyone according to what he has done." (Revelation 22:12) *Vs* "Many will say to me in that day, Lord, Lord, have we not prophesied in thy name? and in thy name have cast out devils? and in thy name done many wonderful works? And then will I profess unto them, I never knew you: depart from me, ye that work iniquity." (Matthew 7:22-23)

Excuse; None available.

Correction: While Jesus in the Bible does not give -any- credit to those who do some good, the Holy Quran shows how God gives us accountability and appreciation:

"That is (the Bounty) whereof Allah gives Glad Tidings to His Servants who believe and do righteous deeds. Say: "No reward do I ask of you for this except the love of those near of kin." And if any one earns any good, We shall give him an increase of good in respect thereof: for Allah is Oft-Forgiving, Most Ready to appreciate (service)." (Quran 42:23)

And

"For He will pay them their wages, nay, He will give them (even) more out of His Bounty: for He is Oft-Forgiving, Most Ready to appreciate (service)." (Quran 35:30)

And

"If you set apart for Allah a goodly portion, He will double it to your (credit), and He will grant you Forgiveness: for Allah is most Ready to appreciate (service), Most Forbearing" (Quran 64:17) (Continued from 160 to 189)

172. <u>The Strong?</u>

Errancy; "May our Lord Jesus Christ himself - encourage your hearts and strengthen you in every good deed and word. (2 Thessalonians 2:16-17) *Vs* "And as they came out, they found a man of Cyrene, Simon by name: him they compelled to bear his cross." (Matthew 27:32)

Note; According to most Bible commentaries, including the Matthew Henry Complete Commentary, the Romans gave the cross to Simon because: 1) it was too heavy for Jesus. 2) The added weight of the cross caused Jesus to swoon and the Romans feared that Jesus might faint or die before reaching the cross.

Excuse; In an attempt to avoid the contradiction in (John 19:17) which does not mention Simon helping Jesus with the cross, apologetics concede that both Simon and Jesus carried the cross because it was too heavy and Jesus was –too weak- to carry the cross.

Rebuttal: It is agreed that Jesus was –too weak- to carry the cross himself for men have weaknesses whereas God does not.

Correction: The Holy Quran shows God has no weakness as in the Bible:

"No just estimate have they made of Allah: for Allah is He Who is strong and able to Carry out His Will." (Quran 22:74)

And

"Allah is gracious unto His servants. He provideth for whom He will. And He is the Strong, the Mighty." (Quran 42:19) (Continued from 160 to 189)

173. <u>The Watchful?</u>

Errancy; "I am the good shepherd; I know my sheep and my sheep know me. He will come in and go out, and find pasture. (John 10:14; 19) *Vs* Jesus unaware of where the body of Lazarus is; "And [Jesus]

said, Where have ye laid him? They said unto him, Lord, come and see."
(John 11:34)

Excuse; Trinitarians concede that because Jesus was in 'flesh-man
form', he could –not- watch everything.

Rebuttal: It is agreed that Jesus could not watch everything as other
Trinitarians attempt to assert.

Correction: The Holy Quran clarifies Allah watches over all of us:

"O people! be careful of (your duty to) your Lord, Who created you
from a single being and created its mate of the same (kind) and spread
from these two, many men and women; and be careful of (your duty to)
Allah, by Whom you demand one of another (your rights), and (to) the
ties of relationship; surely Allah ever watches over you." (Quran 4:1)
(Continued from 160 to 189)

174. Answers Prayers?

Errancy; "You may ask me for anything in my name and I will do it.
(John 14:14) *Vs* Jesus apparently praying to himself or was it to God to
be saved from the cross according to the Trinitarians;

"about the ninth hour Jesus cried with a loud voice, saying, Eli, Eli, lama
sabachthani? That is to say, My God, my God, why hast thou forsaken
me?" (Matthew 27:46)

Excuse; God wanted Jesus to die, which is why the prayers of Jesus to
be saved were not answered.

Rebuttal: Here is where Christian apologetics confuse the Bible even
more. On the one hand, Christians claim Jesus is God, and as we have
read, Jesus obviously wanted to be saved; therefore the Christian's
Triune God wanted to be saved from the cross. However, in order to
explain the contradiction, the Christians try to have it both ways by
saying at that moment, Jesus was not God, and the Real God did not
want Jesus saved. They try to have their cake (sacrifice) and eat it too
(salvation). Christians claim that their trinity is One God, if so, how
could their 'One God' want two different things at that same moment?
Here we uncover their fallacy because you cannot have One God fighting
Himself to live.

Correction: God in the Holy Quran differentiates between the good and bad beings in regards to answering prayers:

"And your Lord says: "Call on Me; I will answer your (Prayer): but those who are too arrogant to serve Me will surely find themselves in Hell - in humiliation!" (Quran 40:60) (Continued from 160 to 189)

175. The Unique?

Errancy; "And the Word was made flesh, and dwelt among us, (and we beheld his glory, the glory as of the only begotten of the Father) full of grace and truth." (John 1:14) *Vs* David 'also' being a begotten son;

"I will declare the decree: the Lord hath said unto me, Thou art my Son; this day have I begotten thee." (Psalms 2:7)

Excuse; Biblical commentaries differ among themselves whether David was a manifestation of Jesus or whether David was –also- a begotten son of God.

Rebuttal: Every time a character in the Bible has attributes equal to or greater than Jesus (Hebrews 7:3-4), apologetics throw away all context for these characters and assert it was another manifestation of Jesus to avoid the fact that Jesus was not unique.

Correction: God in the Quran unlike the Prophets in the Bible shows there is none like Allah, the Unique Creator:

"And your Allah is One Allah: There is no god but He, Most Gracious, Most Merciful." (Quran 2:163) (Continued from 160 to 189)

176. The Last?

Errancy; "I (Jesus) am the first and the last, the Beginning and the Ending." (Revelation 22:13) *Vs* "I have yet many things to say unto you, but ye cannot bear them now. Howbeit when he, the Spirit of truth, is come, he will guide you into all truth: for he shall not speak of himself; but whatsoever he shall hear, that shall he speak: and he will show you things to come." (John 16:12-13)

Note; (John 16:12-13) is considered as one of the many predictions of Prophet Muhammad (peace be upon him) and the Holy Quran as this research makes evident.

Excuse; That is what it says but that is not what it means. This is a prediction about the Holy Spirit, not Muhammad.

Rebuttal: (See Reply letter [E] in Rebuttal Chart). First, Trinitarians claim that the Holy Spirit, God, and Jesus are all one entity while Jesus was obviously speaking of someone other than himself in (John 16:12-13). Jesus spoke about himself in (v12) "I have" then switches from personal pronouns "I" to "he", rather then maintaining a constant personal pronoun of "I". Jesus does not say; "I will come later to finish speaking".

Second, another reason why we know that the Holy Spirit and Jesus are not one in the same is because of (Matthew 12:31);

"Wherefore I say unto you, all manner of sin and blasphemy shall be forgiven unto men: but the blasphemy against the Holy Ghost shall not be forgiven unto men."

Yet after the thief next to Jesus on the cross –mocked and reviled- Jesus (Mark 15:32), Jesus forgave one and said you will go to Heaven (Luke 23:43).

Third, Jesus admits that he has nothing else to say; Jesus states that everything his Creator wanted him to say was already said;

"for all things that I have heard of my Father I have made known unto you." (John 15:15)

Which confirms an individual other than Jesus will say more. For example; it would be a symptom of schizophrenia for someone to say; "I said everything I was told, and I will come to say more from me and I will glorify myself and I will say nothing of my own will other than what I was told by myself".

One has a free choice of following the Trinitarians' entanglement or believing that (John 16:12-13) was the logical prediction of Prophet Muhammad (peace be upon him) because our loving God would not leave us for over 2,000 years with no other guidance.

Correction: God in the Quran states:

"He is the First and the Last, the Evident and the Immanent: and He has full knowledge of all things." (Quran 57:3) (Continued from 160 to 189)

177. **The Equitable?**

Errancy; "This was the true light that gives light to every man who comes into the world." (John 1:9) *Vs* A woman of Canaan when she sought blessings for her daughter:

"But he answered and said, I am sent only to the lost sheep of the house of Israel." (Matthew 15:24)

Even when she asked for help and begged, she was told:

"It is not meet to take the children's bread and to cast it to dogs." (Matthew 15:26)

In the Bible, it shows that eventually, Jesus helped her but after delaying, arguing, and slandering her with the insult "bitch".

Excuse; 1st) that is what it says but that is not what it means. Jesus was using metaphors common towards gentiles (non-Jews). 2nd) Jesus was making an example of her to the disciples that gentiles should be blessed too.

Rebuttal: 1st) (See Reply letter [F] in Rebuttal Chart). Whether a Jew or gentile, such metaphors are insulting and an additional barrier to cross to receive a blessing. The blessing is delayed because of her ethnicity. 2nd) In the Bible, Jesus was obviously not trying to teach anything to his disciples about gentiles other than to continue to avoid them and avoid giving them blessings;

"These twelve Jesus sent forth, and commanded them saying, Go not into the way of the Gentiles, and into any city of the Samaritans enter ye not: But go rather to the lost sheep of the house of Israel." (Matthew 10:5-6)

Even after Jesus departed;

"Now they which were scattered abroad upon the persecution that arose about Stephen traveled as far as Phenice, and Cyprus, and Antioch, preaching the word to none but unto the Jews only." (Acts 11:19)

Correction: God in the Holy Quran is swift in rewarding all people who have sought reward:

"And there are, certainly, among the People of the Book (Jews and Christians), those who believe in Allah, and that which has been revealed to you and in that which has been revealed to them, humbling themselves before Allah: They will not sell the Revelations of Allah for a miserable gain! For them is a reward with their Lord, and Allah is swift in account." (Quran 3:199)

And

"Or do those who have wrought evil deeds think that We shall make them equal with those who believe and do righteous deeds, - that their life and their death shall be equal? Bad is their judgment!" (Quran 45:21) (Continued from 160 to 189)

178. The Gatherer?

Errancy; "Where two or three come together in my name, there am I with them." (Matthew 18:20) and "I have other sheep that are not of this sheep pen. I must bring them also." (John 10:16) *Vs* When an armed group came to apprehend Jesus, the disciples of Jesus instead of staying by the side and security of Christ, instead the disciples, disowned, dispersed and ran away from Christ:

"And they all forsook him, and fled." (Mark 14:50)

Excuse; all those with Jesus were supposed to -scatter away- from him as a fulfillment of prophecy (Zechariah 13:7).

Rebuttal: First, if indeed it was predicted that all the followers of Christ would abandon him, then this prediction confirms Jesus is not a gatherer; instead, the fear of being associated with Christ makes him a disperser. Second, a closer look at (Zechariah 13:7) dispels the notion that the character foretold is Jesus;

"And it shall come to pass, that when any shall yet prophesy, then his father and his mother that begat him shall say unto him, Thou shalt not live; for thou speakest lies in the name of the Lord: and his father and his mother that begat him shall thrust him through when he prophesieth." (Zechariah 13:3)

We see from the preceding passage that the individual foretold was born by a man and woman, while Jesus had no father, second, Mary believed Jesus because angel Gabriel foretold her of Jesus.

In conclusion, whether the desertion by the disciples was foretold or not, in either case, the fact remains that Jesus is not a gatherer, instead he caused many men to flee away from him as was the case with many of the righteous Prophets, who were sent with the message of God, for only God could gather all of the humans, not a messenger.

Correction: Over one billion Muslims gather everyday shoulder to shoulder and foot to foot, to praise our Creator:

"Our Lord! Thou art He that will gather mankind together against a day about which there is no doubt; for Allah never fails in His promise." (Quran 3:9) (Continued from 160 to 189)

179. <u>The Granter of Security?</u>

Errancy; "Satan has asked to sift you as wheat. But I have prayed for you, Simon that your faith may not fail." (Luke 22:31-32) *Vs* "And he was in the wilderness forty days, tempted by Satan" (Mark 1:13, Matthew 4:1, Luke 4:2).

In addition, the Bible states that Jesus was tempted by the Devil in all aspects of his life;

"For we have not a high priest who is unable to sympathize with our weaknesses, but one who in every respect has been tempted as we are, yet without sin." (Hebrews 4:15)

Therefore, Jesus cannot protect us from the Devil when Jesus himself is tempted by Satan.

Excuse; Due to Jesus being in the flesh form, he was susceptible to temptation.

Rebuttal: Here the Trinitarians confess Jesus was tempted, thus contradicting themselves regarding the divinity of Christ because the Bible also says God cannot be tempted;

"Let no one say when he is tempted, "I am tempted by God"; for God cannot be tempted with evil and he himself tempts no one" (James 1:13)

In conclusion, the Trinitarians are repeatedly telling us that Jesus is God while in the process; they are creating even more contradictions with in the Bible. Jesus by the characterization of his temptation cannot protect us from Satan when Christ himself is enticed.

Correction: God, the Holy One in the Quran is our True Protector:

"Secret counsels are only (inspired) by the Devil, in order that he may cause grief to the Believers; but he cannot harm them in the least, except as Allah permits; and on Allah let the Believers put their trust." (Quran 58:10) (Continued from 160 to 189)

180. The Guide?

Errancy; "He calls his own sheep by name and leads them out. When he has brought out all his own, he goes on ahead of them, and his sheep follow him because they know his voice. (John 10:3-4) *Vs* "Then Jesus ordered his disciples not to tell anyone that he was the Messiah." (Matthew 16:20; 8:4, 17:9, Mark 7:36, 8:30, 9:9, Luke 5:14, 8:56, 9:21).

Excuse; 1st) you must understand the context of the verse. Jesus did not want to tell anyone until he rose from the dead. 2nd) Jesus did not want to be overwhelmed with followers (Mark 7:36)

Rebuttal: 1st) Jesus, In the Bible, contradicted his own command because he told some that he was the Messiah before the crucifixion;

"The woman saith to him, I know that Messiah cometh, which is called Christ: when he is come, he will tell us all things. Jesus saith to her, I that speak to thee am he." (John 4:25-26)

And

"But he held his peace, and answered nothing. Again, the high priest asked him, and said to him, Art thou the Christ, the Son of the Blessed? And Jesus said, I am...." (Mark 14:61-62)

Therefore the first excuse is invalidated because in the Bible, Jesus himself contradicted that command and excuse and did not ask or prevent the woman he confessed to from telling others (John 4:28-29).

2nd) If Jesus did not want to be overwhelmed with followers, then this also invalidates him as an ultimate and true source of guidance because the True Guide wants everyone to know the Truth.

Correction: God in the Quran is the True Guide:

175

"Thus have We made for every prophet an enemy among the sinners: but enough is thy Lord to guide and to help." (Quran 25:31) (Continued from 160 to 189)

181. The Patient?

Errancy; "I was shown mercy so that in me, the worst of sinners Christ Jesus might display his unlimited patience as an example for those who would believe on him and receive eternal life." (1 Timothy 1:16) *Vs* Jesus showing an extreme lack of patience by supposedly cursing a fig tree for not producing fruit out of season;

"he [Jesus] felt hungry, and, noticing in the distance a fig-tree in leaf, he went to see if he could find anything on it. But when he came there he found nothing but leaves; for it was not the season for figs" (Mark 11:12-14).

Excuse; That is what it says but that is not what it means. The fig tree symbolizes Israel and Jesus was frustrated and cursed Israel for not producing fruit.

Rebuttal: (See Reply letter [E] in Rebuttal Chart). There are multiple errors with this excuse besides it's admission that Jesus is not patient. First, as we know at this point, Jesus told his disciples not to preach to Israel yet, so it is illogical to curse Israel before Jesus even tries to save Israel. Second, the phrase "not yet in season" would also conflict with the excuse that the fig tree is a metaphor for Israel. As Biblical commentaries confess, Jesus was simply hungry and –could not wait-.

Correction: God in the Holy Quran does not become inpatient as Jesus does. God is characterized in the Quran by infinite patience:

"If Allah were to punish men according to what they deserve. He would not leave on the back of the (earth) a single living creature: but He gives them respite for a stated Term: when their Term expires, verily Allah has in His sight all His Servants." (Quran 35:45)

And

"O ye who believe! seek help with patient perseverance and prayer; for Allah is with those who patiently persevere." (Quran 2:153) (Continued from 160 to 189)

182. The Hidden?

Errancy; "And God said, Thou canst not see my face: for there shall no man see me, and live." (Exodus 33:20) and "No man hath seen God at any time" (John 1:18) *Vs* "Jesus answered him, I spake openly to the world; I ever taught in the synagogue, and in the temple, whither the Jews always resort; and in secret have I said nothing." (John 18:20)

Excuse; Jesus was not God on earth.

Rebuttal: Agreed; nor is Jesus (God) in Heaven because God does not lose the "status" of being God wherever God is (Joshua 2:11).

Correction: The Holy Quran corrects this conflict in the Bible:

"He is the First and the Last and the Ascendant (over all) and the Hidden, and He is Cognizant of all things." (Quran 57:3) (Continued from 160 to 189)

183. The Provider?

Errancy; "I am the bread of life. He who comes to me will never go hungry, and he who believes in me will never be thirsty. (John 6:35) *Vs* Jesus in a major contradiction does not even provide for himself when he is –hungry-;

"he [Jesus] felt hungry, and, noticing in the distance a fig-tree in leaf, he went to see if he could find anything on it. But when he came there he found nothing but leaves; for it was not the season for figs" (Mark 11:12-14).

Excuse; 1st) That is what it says but that is not what it means. The fig tree symbolizes Israel and Jesus was frustrated and cursed Israel for not producing fruit. 2nd) Jesus was speaking of spiritual hunger, not physical hunger.

Rebuttal: 1st) (See Reply letter [E] in Rebuttal Chart). There are multiple errors with this excuse besides it's admission that Jesus does not feed his own hunger for as we all know God is Self Sufficient. First, as we know at this point, Jesus told his disciples not to preach to Israel yet, so it is illogical to curse Israel before Jesus even tries to save Israel. Second, the phrase "not yet in season" would also conflict with the excuse that the fig tree is a metaphor for Israel. As Biblical commentaries confess, Jesus was simply hungry and –could not wait-;

Third, instead of making the tree bear fruit, Jesus cursed it so that it would not feed his hunger or the hunger of his disciples ever again.

2nd) Jesus also lacked to provide himself with spiritual hunger as well in the Bible for after passionate praying, Jesus says;

"And about the ninth hour Jesus cried with a loud voice, saying, Eli, Eli, lama sabachthani? that is to say, My God, my God, why hast thou forsaken me?" (Matthew 27:46)

Furthermore, physical hunger is in fact intertwined with spiritual hunger, as Jesus uses food as metaphors, Jesus also goes in the desert to abstain from food as a spiritual challenge;

"Then was Jesus led up of the Spirit into the wilderness to be tempted of the devil. And when he had fasted forty days and nights, Jesus was hungry." (Matthew 4:1-2)

Correction: We see in the Quran that God is the Provider for everyone, including Jesus (Quran 4:157):

"No Sustenance do I require of them, nor do I require that they should feed Me. For Allah is He Who gives (all) Sustenance, - Lord of Power, - Steadfast (for ever)." (Quran 51:57-58)

Here Allah clarifies that He does not need any food from any creature (including trees), and Allah is the one who provides contentment to all. Furthermore, the context of these verses implies the "sustenance" can be spiritual or physical: "Woe, then, to the Unbelievers..." (Quran 51:60) (Continued from 160 to 189)

184. <u>The Everlasting?</u>

Errancy; "Jesus Christ the same yesterday, and to day, and for ever." (Hebrews 13:8) *Vs* We see that Jesus the man ceased to exist;

"With a loud cry Jesus died." (Mark 15:37)

Excuse; Jesus had to die to fulfill scripture.

Rebuttal: This confirms Jesus was not everlasting, which affirms that as a man, Jesus was not God.

Correction: The Holy Quran describes a True Everlasting God:

"Allah! There is no god but He,-the Living, the Self-subsisting, Eternal. No slumber can seize Him nor sleep." (Quran 2:255)

Therefore, not only does God in the Quran not die, but God does not even sleep!

And

"Allah! There is no god but He,-the Living, the Self-Subsisting, Eternal." (Quran 3:2)

And

"And put thy trust in Him Who lives and dies not; and celebrate his praise; and enough is He to be acquainted with the faults of His servants" (Quran 25:58) (Continued from 160 to 189)

185. God Afraid of us?

Errancy; "If thou wilt not observe to do all the words of this law that are written in this book, that thou mayest fear this glorious and fearful name, The Lord Thy God; Then the Lord will make thy plagues wonderful, and the plagues of thy seed, even great plagues, and of long continuance, and sore sicknesses, and of long continuance." (Deuteronomy 28:58-59)

And

Jesus speaking about himself according to Trinitarians;

"And fear not them which kill the body, but are not able to kill the soul: but rather fear Him which is able to destroy both soul and body in hell." (Matthew 10:28, Luke 8:50, 12:4)

Vs

"After these things Jesus walked in Galilee: for he would not walk in Jewry, because the Jews sought to kill him." (John 7:1)

"Then they took up stones to cast at him: but Jesus hid himself, and went out of the temple, going through the midst of them, and so passed by." (John 8:59)

And

"While ye have light, believe in the light, that ye may be the children of light. These things spake Jesus, and departed, and did hide himself from them." (John 12:36-37)

From childhood, Jesus hid over 10 years in Egypt to avoid death;

"Now when they were departed, behold, an angel of the Lord appeareth to Joseph in a dream, saying, Arise and take the young child and his mother, and flee into Egypt, and be thou there until I tell thee: for Herod will seek the young child to destroy him." (Matthew 2:13)

Excuse; 1st) It was not yet his time to die; "My hour has not yet come" (John 2:4; 8:20)

Rebuttal: Sacrificial lambs are supposed to be killed in their childhood;

"Your lamb must be a one-year-old male without any defects." (Exodus 12:5)

We know that Jesus escaped from death during his childhood (Matthew 2:13)

Second, even when it was his so-called time, Jesus, displayed intense fear, crying out twice;

"Jesus again gave a loud cry and breathed his last." (Matthew 27:50)

In conclusion, whether Jesus was supposed to die as a child or as an adult, every effort was made by him to avoid death.

Correction: Unlike the Bible, the Quran exhibits a Fearless God;

"O Prophet! Fear Allah, and hearken not to the Unbelievers and the Hypocrites: verily Allah is full of Knowledge and Wisdom." (Quran 33:1)

"O Ye who believe! Put not yourselves forward before Allah and His Messenger; but fear Allah: for Allah is He Who hears and knows all things." (Quran 49:1) (Continued from 160 to 189)

186. Begets?

Errancy; Christians claim that God sired Himself;

"God said to Jesus,' You are my son today I have begotten you" (Hebrews 5:5)

Excuse; Mistranslation.

Rebuttal: (See Reply letter [I] in Rebuttal Chart)

Correction: God is unlike any other as the Quran shows us:

"Say: He is Allah, The One; Allah, the Eternal Absolute; He does Not Beget, Nor is He Begotten, and there is None Like unto Him." (Quran 112:1) (Continued from 160 to 189)

187. Trinitarians Lazy?

Errancy; Trinitarians claim that we no longer have to do the work God commanded us to do. Their reasoning is that (1) we could not do the laws (Romans 3:10) and (2) Jesus was God, and his death on the cross removed past and future sin, so there's –no longer- any reason to follow the millenniums old, Laws of God;

"For Christ has brought the Law to an end, so that everyone who believes is put right with God." (Romans 10:4)

"Yet we know that a person is put right with God only through faith in Jesus Christ, never by doing what the Law requires." (Galatians 2:16)

And

"And so the Law was in charge of us until Christ came, in order that we might then be put right with God through faith." (Galatians 3:24)

Vs

As we have already shown, and as Trinitarians (contradicting themselves) say, "Jesus was not God on earth". Besides the divine disqualification for Jesus to replace the laws or remove the sins associated with the laws, there is another obstacle for Trinitarians to claim the laws are "too hard" for us to accomplish;

"you will have to obey him and keep all his laws that are written in this book of his teachings. You will have to turn to him with all your heart. The command that I am giving you today is not too difficult or beyond your reach. It is not up in the sky. You do not have to ask, "Who will go up and bring it down for us, so that we can hear it and obey it?' Nor is it on the other side of the ocean. You do not have to ask, "Who will go across the ocean and bring it to us, so that we may hear it and obey it?' No, it is here with you. You know it and can quote it, so now obey it."

"Today I am giving you a choice between good and evil, between life and death. If you obey the commands of the Lord your God, which I give you today, if you love him, obey him, and keep all his laws, then you will prosper and become a nation of many people. The Lord your God will bless you in the land that you are about to occupy. But if you disobey and refuse to listen, and are led away to worship other gods, you will be destroyed—I warn you here and now. You will not live long in that land across the Jordan that you are about to occupy." (Deuteronomy 30:10-18)

Furthermore, Jesus promised many people would be in Heaven before he supposedly ended the Law through his claimed resurrection;

"So then, whoever disobeys even the least important of the commandments and teaches others to do the same, will be least in the Kingdom of heaven. On the other hand, whoever obeys the Law and teaches others to do the same, will be great in the Kingdom of heaven." (Matthew 5:19)

"Happy are those who are persecuted because they do what God requires; the Kingdom of heaven belongs to them!" (Matthew 5:10)

"Happy are those who know they are spiritually poor; the Kingdom of heaven belongs to them!" (Matthew 5:3)

"but Jesus said, "Let the children come to me, and do not hinder them; for to such belongs the kingdom of heaven." (Matthew 19:14)

Last, Jesus himself taught that following the commandments and the laws is the way to salvation;

"Not every one that saith unto me, Lord, Lord, shall enter into the kingdom of heaven; but he that doeth the will of my Father which is in heaven." (Matthew 7:21)

Excuse; The laws were supposed to be followed until the resurrection, after the resurrection, the laws were done away with;

"Purge out therefore the old leaven, that ye may be a new lump, as ye are unleavened. For even Christ our Passover is sacrificed for us" (1 Corinthians 5:7)

Rebuttal: It is a faulty notion to claim the laws, which were followed for millenniums, were only made to be temporary. Both the God of Abraham and Jesus state the laws are forever;

"Everlasting" ,"For All Generations", "a Perpetual Ordinance " (Exodus 27:21; 28:43; 29:28; 30:21; 31:17; Leviticus 6:18, 22; 7:34, 36; 10:9, 15; 17:7; 23:14, 21, 41; 24:3; Numbers 10:8; 15:15; 18:8, 11, 19, 23; 19:10; Deuteronomy 5:29; Psalms 119:160) and is Not to be changed or taken away from (Deuteronomy 4:2; 12:32).

Jesus confirms the Laws are for all generations and everlasting by following the laws (Matthew 8:4, 26:19, John 7:10).

Actions speak louder than words and besides the actions of Jesus keeping the Everlasting Laws, Jesus also states;

"Think not that I am come to destroy the law, or the prophets: I am not come to destroy, but to fulfill. For verily I say unto you, Till heaven and earth pass, one jot or one title shall in no wise pass from the law, till all be fulfilled." (Matthew 5:17-18)

In conclusion, God, the Prophets, and the Messiah all say the Laws are unending. The Righteous have one enemy, he who leads people astray through lethargy.

Correction: God through the Holy Quran explains that it is a combination of Faith and Works that gives us Salvation:

"For Him (alone) is prayer in Truth: any others that they call upon besides Him hear them no more than if they were to stretch forth their hands for water to reach their mouths but it reaches them not: for the prayer of those without Faith is nothing but (futile) wandering (in the mind)." (Quran 13:14)

The Holy Quran explains that works are to our benefit:

"O you whose hearts have been touched with the divine hand: When you intend to stand before God for performing your act of worship, then ablution becomes a duty. Wash your faces, your hands and the forearms up to the elbows, and with your wet hands wipe your heads, then wash your feet to the ankles...God does not intend to put you in difficulty but only to make you sound headed men of proper discipline and excellent mind, and to set you upon a course of purity of thought and action, for the actions of men are best interpreters of their thoughts, and He means to make all grace abound in you that you may hopefully actuate yourselves with the feeling of gratitude and gratefulness and lift Him your inward sight." (Quran 5:6) (Continued from 160 to 189)

188. The Word?

Errancy; "In the beginning the Word already existed; the Word was with God, and the Word was God." (John 1:1)

And

"The Word became a human being and, full of grace and truth, lived among us. We saw his glory, the glory which he received as the Father's only Son." (John 1:14)

Vs

"Every good gift and every perfect present comes from heaven; it comes down from God, the Creator of the heavenly lights, who does not change or cause darkness by turning." (James 1:17)

Excuse; That is what it says but that is not what it means. This is speaking of God's essence, not changing into a man.

Rebuttal: (See Reply letter [E] in Rebuttal Chart) Bible scholars have confused a miracle by God into a creation of God.

"The Word" in context from the Bible delineates the method used by God to create life;

"And God (said), Let there (be) light: and there was light." (Genesis 1:3)

With a word, God created our planet's source of energy, the sun. The sun and the word of God became one; that does not mean we worship the sun, nor does it mean that the sun is God as ancient cultures believed.

We see again that God creates many living creatures besides Jesus with a "word";

"Then God commanded, "Let the water be filled with many kinds of living beings, and let the air be filled with birds." (Genesis 1:20)

Unlike the people of pharaoh, we do not worship figures. If we follow the logic of the Trinitarians, those created with the "word" are considered divine.

Therefore, we see in the framework of the Bible, that the word becoming flesh is a commonplace action and does not denote divinity.

Correction: The Holy Quran clarifies this point perfectly by stating:

"She said: My Lord! when shall there be a son (born) to I me, and man has not touched me? He said: Even so, Allah creates what He pleases; when He has decreed a matter, He only says to it, (Be), and it is." (Quran 3:47)

"The similitude of Jesus before Allah is as that of Adam; He created him from dust, then said to him: "Be". And he was." (Quran 3:59)
(Continued from 160 to 189)

189. Worshipping a man?

Errancy; The majority of Christians believe that Jesus is God in flesh form, hence these Christians worship Jesus. These Christians validate worshipping Jesus, through the following verses;

"And when they were come into the house, they saw the young child with Mary his mother, and fell down, and worshipped him: and when they had opened their treasures, they presented unto him gifts; gold, and frankincense, and myrrh." (Matthew 2:11)

"And as they went to tell his disciples, behold, Jesus met them, saying, All hail. And they came and held him by the feet, and worshipped him." (Matthew 28:9)

"And changed the glory of the incorruptible God into an image made like to corruptible man" (Romans 1:23)

Yet the Bible also says;

"I am the Lord, that is my name; my glory I give to no other, nor my praise to graven images." (Isaiah 42:8)

And

"For I am the Lord; I change not." (Malachi 3:6)

And

"God is not a man, that he should lie; neither the son of man, that he should repent." (Numbers 23:19)

Excuse; None available.

Correction: The confusion of whether to worship or not to worship a man is resolved through the Quran:

"And behold! Allah will say "O Jesus the son of Mary! didst thou say unto men `worship me and my mother as gods in derogation of Allah?" He will say: "Glory to Thee! never could I say what I had no right (to say). Had I said such a thing Thou wouldst indeed have known it. Thou knowest what is in my heart though I know not what is in Thine. For Thou knowest in full all that is hidden."

Clearly, we should only worship God and God alone.

"Never said I to them aught except what Thou didst command me to say to wit `Worship Allah my Lord and your Lord'; and I was a witness over them whilst I dwelt amongst them; when Thou didst take me up thou wast the Watcher over them and Thou art a Witness to all things." (Quran 5:116-117)

In conclusion, the Trinitarians propagate that Jesus, the Holy Spirit, and God are all 100% equal, and are all a part of the triune God. These Christians try to justify this notion with the mathematical equation ($1 \times 1 \times 1 = 1$) yet according to the excuses of the Bible scholars; the value of Jesus is not completely equal to God.

By their own admission, Jesus on earth was ($<$) less than God in heaven.

Therefore, the actual equation is ($.5 \times .5 \times 1 = .25$) Symbolically, by claiming Jesus is a part of a trinity, the triune god becomes a fraction.

(IX.) AFTERLIFE

190. How to remove Sin

Errancy; Christians claim the only way to salvation is through blood; "For the life of the flesh is in the blood: and I have given it to you upon the altar to make an atonement for your souls: for it is the blood that maketh an atonement for the soul." (Leviticus 17:11)

Vs

Multiple methods of removing sin; giving charity (Exodus 30:15-16) and (Numbers 31:50), incense (Numbers 16:46-47)

Excuse; None available.

Correction: Islam teaches that there is no one single way to salvation for salvation comes from both works and faith:

"For Him (alone) is prayer in Truth: any others that they call upon besides Him hear them no more than if they were to stretch forth their hands for water to reach their mouths but it reaches them not: for the prayer of those without Faith is nothing but (futile) wandering (in the mind)." (Quran 13:14)

"They will say: "Did there not come to you your messengers with Clear Signs?" They will say, "Yes". They will reply, "Then pray (as ye like)! But the prayer of those without Faith is nothing but (futile wandering) in (mazes of) error!" (Quran 40:50)

"Those who believe, and do deeds of righteousness, and establish regular prayers and regular charity, will have their reward with their Lord: on them shall be no fear, nor shall they grieve." (Quran 2:277)

191. Born sinners?

Errancy; Children are born pure, without sin (Leviticus 11:44, 19:2, 20:7) *Vs* Children are born wicked sinners (Psalms 58:3)

Excuse; That is what it says but that is not what it means. (Psalms 58:3) is speaking about the potential to commit sin, not being an actual sinner.

Rebuttal: (See Reply letter [E] in Rebuttal Chart). The language and context used is that of one who is a sinner, not of one who will be a sinner.

"The wicked are estranged from the womb" -not- "will be" (future tense), instead "are" (present tense)

"they go astray as soon as they be born, speaking lies."

not will go astray as adults.

Furthermore, Paul also adopts the absurdity that children are sinners by claiming;

"Wherefore, as by one man sin entered into the world, and death by sin; and so death passed upon all men, for that all have sinned" (Romans 5:12)

Correction: The Quran corrects the fallacy that children are inherently evil or have contracted sin of previous generations;

"We have indeed created man in the best of moulds." (Quran 95:4)

"Every soul draws the wages of its acts on none But itself: no bearer of burdens can bear The burden of another." (Quran 6:164)

"…No laden soul will bear another's load. Then unto your Lord is your return; and He will tell you what ye used to do. Lo! He knoweth what is in the breasts (of men)." (Quran 39:7)

192. Equal Reward?

Errancy; Jesus giving a parable of Heaven says that those who work harder for their reward will be equal to those who work less (Matthew 20:1-16) *Vs* "And, behold, I come quickly; and my reward is with me, to give every man according as his work" (Revelation 22:12)

Excuse; That is what it says but that is not what it means. Some people do not have the opportunity to work as hard as others do, that is why in (Matthew 20), both were rewarded equally.

Rebuttal: (See Reply letter [E] in Rebuttal Chart). The workers who only worked for one hour compared to those who worked for nine hours had the same opportunity to work as many hours as they would like but the one hour workers were not as inspired or motivated to find salvation as the ones who worked nine hours;

"For the kingdom of heaven is like unto a man that is an householder, which went out early in the morning to hire labourers into his vineyard." (Matthew 20:1)

Here we see that the house owner went out "early in the morning" and found the workers who worked nine hours ready and willing to be saved. As the early bird catches the food, so may those who eagerly seek God's Mercy.

As for the workers who only worked one hour;

"And about the eleventh hour he went out, and found others standing idle" (Matthew 20:6)

These one-hour workers did not bother to search for work until hours later, perhaps after a sinful day, and they only worked because of necessity rather than voluntarily as the morning workers. Thus we see both workers had the same opportunity to wake up early, but the ones who reluctantly worked were unfairly rewarded the same as those who readily worked.

Correction: The Quran uplifts the Bible in that God is a fair Judge who gives us accountability:

"Surely Allah does not do injustice to the weight of an atom, and if it is a good deed He multiplies it and gives from Himself a great reward." (Quran 4:40)

193. <u>Who is Satan?</u>

Errancy; There is confusion in the Bible as to whether Satan is a fallen angel or not;

Satan is free to act as he pleases (Job 1:6-7, 2:1-2, Matthew 4:1, 1 Pet 5:8) *Vs* The angels who rebelled against God are chained up (Jude 6)

Excuse; 1st) That is what it says but that is not what it means. The angels will be ultimately bound in the future, but are not yet actually bound;

"And, behold, they cried out, saying, What have we to do with thee, Jesus, thou Son of God? art thou come hither to torment us before the time?" (Matthew 8:29)

2nd) There are two different types of fallen angels, those in chains and those not.

Rebuttal: 1st) (See Reply letter [E] in Rebuttal Chart). Here the Bible scholars attempt another word play by confusing the past, current and future tense of the passages;

"For if God spared not the angels that sinned, but cast them down to hell, and delivered them into chains of darkness, to be reserved unto judgment" (2 Peter 2:4)

We see the past tense verbs are "spared not, sinned, cast them down, delivered, and reserved"

It is obvious to any reader that the fallen angels were thrown out past tense, are chained up current tense, and will be judged future tense.

2nd) "...spared not the angels that sinned..." (2 Peter 2:4) proves that none of the angels who sinned were spared, instead of some of the angels as the apologetics suggest. Nothing suggests that there are two different types of fallen angels except for the contradiction that evil angels are free to roam and yet at the same time are chained up.

Correction: The Noble Quran specifies that Satan was a Jinn (a separate breed of creatures made from fire (15:27), not an Angel:

"Behold! We said to the angels, "Bow down to Adam": They bowed down except Iblis. He was one of the Jinns, and he broke the Command of his Lord. Will ye then take him and his progeny as protectors rather than Me? And they are enemies to you! Evil would be the exchange for the wrong-doers!" (Quran 18:50)

194. Untouched Males?

Errancy; In an affront to 99% of humans world wide, the Bible makes an incongruous declaration that only a certain race, and certain gender, and certain marital status will be in front of God;

"the hundred and forty and four thousand, which were redeemed from the earth. These are they which were -not defiled with women-; for they are virgins." (Revelation 14:3-4)

Excuse; None available.

Correction: The Holy Quran corrects this limitation of those who have the opportunity to go to Heaven by bluntly stating that Heaven is open for all and any who strive for it:

"If any do deeds of righteousness, - be they male or female - and have faith, they will enter Heaven, and not the least injustice will be done to them." (Quran 4:124)

Furthermore, being with a woman in a marital relationship is actually a blessing, not a defilement:

"Permitted to you, on the night of the fasts, is the approach to your wives. They are your garments and ye are their garments." (Quran 2:187)

195. Poor a Curse?

Errancy; Have wealth to pass along to your grandchildren (Proverbs 13:22, 1 Timothy 5:8) *Vs* Do not have any wealth (Matthew 6:19)

Excuse; Jesus never said to give it all away;

Rebuttal: Wrong, Jesus did say to "give it –all- away"; when a righteous person who kept all the commandments (Luke 18:21) asked Jesus how to attain eternal life, Jesus replied that the one single thing he lacked was;

"Yet lackest thou one thing: sell all that thou hast, and distribute unto the poor, and thou shalt have treasure in heaven" (Luke 18:22)

Furthermore, in regards to storing treasures on earth, Jesus says;

"And again I say unto you, it is easier for a camel to go through the eye of a needle, than for a rich man to enter into the kingdom of God." (Matthew 19:24)

Peter confirms that the disciples gave away all they had;

"Then answered Peter and said unto him, Behold, we have forsaken –all-, and followed thee; what shall we have therefore?" (Matthew 19:27)

And Jesus again reaffirms that for giving away all they had, they will be rewarded in Heaven;

"Jesus said to them, "You can be sure that when the Son of Man sits on his glorious throne in the New Age, then you twelve followers of mine will also sit on thrones, to rule the twelve tribes of Israel." (Matthew 19:28)

Therefore, we have a direct contradiction where Paul teaches to store treasures while Jesus teaches the righteous to give it all away.

Correction: Being poor or rich in the Holy Quran is not a barometer of your righteousness, for we are meant to be tested with both poverty and riches:

"Be sure we shall test you with something of fear and hunger, some loss in goods or lives or the fruits (of your toil), but give glad tidings to those who patiently persevere" (Quran 2:155)

And

"That which is on earth we have made but as a glittering show for the earth, in order that We may test them - as to which of them are best in conduct." (Quran 18:7)

We are given many trials and tribulations and our Ultimate Treasure is in Heaven. Therefore being poor is not a curse nor are we damned because we don't have to have so much money as to afford to "take care" of our grandchildren (Proverbs 13:22).

196. Reap what you sow?

Errancy; Some sow wheat but reap thorns. (Jeremiah 12:13) *Vs* Some sow but will not reap anything. (Micah 6:15) *Vs* Some reap without sowing. (Matthew 25:26, Luke 19:22) *Vs* A man reaps what he sows. (2 Corinthians 9:6, Galatians 6:7)

Excuse; The first are materialistic sowing, thus uneven, the last is afterlife spiritual sowing, thus even.

Rebuttal: This would be acceptable albeit for the passage stating that the righteous reap what they sow in this life, hence materialistic terms;

"Behold, the righteous shall be recompensed in the earth: much more the wicked and the sinner." (Proverbs 11:31) because (Matthew 25:26, Luke 19:22) speaks of the wicked materialistically getting more than the righteous.

Therefore, even if it is in materialistic terms, it is in contradiction to (Proverbs 11:31)

Correction: The Quran is very clear that humans get what they deserve. In an accountable fashion, God is Fair and Bountiful. People are punished for the bad and greatly rewarded for the good:

"Surely Allah does not do injustice to the weight of an atom, and if it is a good deed He multiplies it and gives from Himself a great reward." (Quran 4:40)

197. Righteous Immortal?

Errancy; The righteous in the Bible are immortal; "No grave trouble will overtake the righteous" (Proverbs 12:21) *Vs* the righteous in the Bible are mortal;

"…How can ye escape the damnation of Hell? Wherefore, behold, I send unto you prophets, and wise men, and scribes: and some of them ye shall kill and crucify; and some of them shall ye scourge in your synagogues, and persecute them from city to city: That upon you may come all the righteous blood shed upon the earth, from the blood of Innocent Abel unto the blood of Zacharias son of Barachias, whom ye slew between the temple and the altar. Verily I say unto you, All these things shall come upon this generation." (Matthew 23:33-36)

Excuse; (Proverbs 12:21) is speaking about only a few righteous people, not all righteous people.

Rebuttal: We know that the Bible has universally taught the false concept that the righteous are immortal. This is based from other passages stating such;

"They shall take up serpents; and if they drink any deadly thing, it shall not hurt them; they shall lay hands on the sick, and they shall recover." (Mark 16:18)

In an affront to Bible defenders, Mark teaches that all the righteous can drink snake venom and survive, avoiding death. This is a direct contradiction with all the righteous recorded in the Bible who have died.

Correction: The Quran clarifies that all humans, good or bad, are not immortal:

"Say: "Running away will not profit you if ye are running away from death or slaughter..." (Quran 33:16)

"We have ordained death among you and We are not to be outrun" (Quran 56:60)

Medicine and machines may have the ability to slow the process of death, by the Will of God but eventually as described in the Quran, we all will die, and the angel of death will come to all of us and we will not be able to prevent the angel from taking us away from this earth.

198. Light in Hell?

Errancy; Hell is a place of darkness (Matthew 8:12) *Vs* Hell is a place of light (Mark 9:48)

Excuse; That is what it says but that is not what it means. Fire means a place of destruction and darkness means a place of lost ones.

Rebuttal: (See Reply letter [E] in Rebuttal Chart). We know that when the Bible is speaking of fire, that it means literal fire because in another passage, a man in Hell says;

"...dip the tip of his finger in water, and cool my tongue; for I am tormented in this flame." (Luke 16:24)

Again, we know that this passage is speaking literally of a flaming fire from this quote;

"These two were thrown alive into the lake of fire that burns with sulphur." (Revelation 19:20)

Correction: Hell is indeed a place full of flames, and the Quran clarifies that the darkness Jesus is referring to is the molten liquid poured on the evil doers:

"Yea, such! - then shall they taste it, - a boiling fluid, and a fluid dark, murky, intensely cold!-" (Quran 38:57)

Therefore, instead of Biblical apologetics trying to change word meanings or trying to think metaphorically instead of using literal logic, the Quran explains that the liquid used is dark, like the crust and smoke from lava.

"(It is) the Fire of (the Wrath of) Allah kindled (to a blaze)," (Quran 104:6)

A kindling blaze is the location of hell and a boiling dark is the liquid will meet the evil doers in the location. Thus, it is literally detailed in the Holy Quran.

199. One More Chance?

Errancy; The Bible claims that once a believer loses faith, he or she can never return to God;

"For how can those who abandon their faith be brought back to repent again? They were once in God's light; they tasted heaven's gift and received their share of the Holy Spirit; they knew from experience that God's word is good, and they had felt the powers of the coming age. And then they abandoned their faith! It is impossible to bring them back to repent again, because they are again crucifying the Son of God and exposing him to public shame." (Hebrews 6:4-6)

Excuse; Biblical theologians differ in their interpretation of these passages, some concede that salvation can be lost, others claim it is a mistranslation; 'fall away' should be 'drift way' indicating there is still hope.

Rebuttal: (See Reply letter [I] in Rebuttal Chart). Whether [fall away or drift away], it is still "impossible" for one (v4) to return. Therefore, those apologetics offer false hope by ignoring the context.

Correction: The Holy Quran acknowledges that people do "fall" or "drift" away from their religion, yet the Quran does not abandon people's hopes as the Bible does, the Holy Quran explains that God gives us more than a single chance to repent and be saved:

"Those who believe, then reject faith, then believe (again) and (again) reject faith, and go on increasing in unbelief,- Allah will not forgive them nor guide them nor guide them on the way." (Quran 4:137)

In the Quran, those who drift away are given another chance. Unlike in the Bible, those who go astray from the straight path, even once, are not able to return back to God.

200. <u>Saved Forever?</u>

Errancy; The Bible claims that salvation can be lost; "For how can those who abandon their faith be brought back to repent again? They were once in God's light; they tasted heaven's gift and received their share of the Holy Spirit; they knew from experience that God's word is good, and they had felt the powers of the coming age. And then they abandoned their faith! It is impossible to bring them back to repent again, because they are again crucifying the Son of God and exposing him to public shame." (Hebrews 6:4-6)

Yet elsewhere, the Bible says salvation is permanent;

"And I give unto them eternal life; and they shall never perish, neither shall any man pluck them out of my hand." (John 10:28, Romans 8:38-39, Ephesians 1:13)

Excuse; Biblical theologians differ in their interpretation of these passages for some concede that salvation can be lost, others claim it is a mistranslation; 'fall away' should be 'drift way' indicating there is still hope.

Rebuttal: (See Reply letter [I] in Rebuttal Chart). Whether [fall away or drift away], you are still –away-, hence it is possible to lose salvation as other parts of the Bible confirm;

"But when the righteous turneth away from his righteousness, and committeth iniquity, and doeth according to all the abominations that the wicked man doeth, shall he live? All his righteousness that he hath done shall not be mentioned: in his trespass that he hath trespassed, and in his sin that he hath sinned, in them shall he die." (Ezekiel 18:24)

And

"For if after they have escaped the pollutions of the world through the knowledge of the Lord and Savior Jesus Christ, they are again entangled therein, and overcome, the latter end is worse with them than the beginning. For it had been better for them not to have known the way of righteousness, than, after they have known it, to turn from the holy commandment delivered unto them." (2 Peter 2:20-21)

These two additional passages, besides proving that a believer can go astray, also go a step further by stating that apostates will suffer or even be killed. Their eternal destiny changes because they are no longer delivered and all their righteousness is erased.

Correction: The Holy Quran affirms without contradiction that people do "fall" or "drift" away from their religion. Salvation is a lifetime goal. The Quran is not as discarding as the Bible, the Holy Quran explains that God gives us more than a single chance to repent and return:

"Those who believe, then reject faith, then believe (again) and (again) reject faith, and go on increasing in unbelief,- Allah will not forgive them nor guide them nor guide them on the way." (Quran 4:137)

Additional Ways

201. <u>Rewarded on Earth or in Heaven?</u>

Errancy; "Behold, the righteous shall be recompensed in the earth: much more the wicked and the sinner." (Proverbs 11:31) *Vs* "Jesus said unto him, If thou wilt be perfect, go and sell that thou hast, and give to the poor, and thou shalt have treasure in heaven" (Matthew 19:21, 1 Corinthians 3:12–15, Revelation 22:12).

Excuse; Rewards begin on earth and are completed in Heaven.

Rebuttal: This is an assumption with no basis. A fabricated and unsubstantiated notion. Many believers suffer in this life without rewards. Furthermore, many righteous people have far less than the wicked.

Therefore, to guarantee that reward begins in this life is a lie and impossibility. Even if a partial reward began on earth, it does not quell the statement that the righteous will have -more reward- than the wicked -on earth-.

Paul himself is one who suffered a torturous death in this life assuming he will instead be rewarded in the next (Acts 14:19).

In fact, Paul says that the righteous "suffer" in this life (not rewarded) and instead will be rewarded in the next life, therefore discrediting the claim that we will be rewarded more than the wicked in this life for being righteous;

"If we suffer, we shall also reign with him" (2 Timothy 2:12)

In a complete contradiction to Solomon, Paul says the righteous are guaranteed to suffer, -not- be rewarded on earth;

"Yea, and all that will live godly in Christ Jesus shall suffer persecution." (2 Timothy 3:12)

Correction: The Holy Quran does not make the unrealistic claim that the treasures of earth are a reflection of one's righteousness. Instead, the Holy Quran explains that some receive rewards in this life as a test for the more important and everlasting life, the Afterlife:

"God is the One who increases the provision for whomever He wills, or withholds it. They have become preoccupied with this life; and this life, compared to the Hereafter, is nothing." (Quran 13:26)

"It is He Who hath made you (His) agents, inheritors of the earth: He hath raised you in ranks, some above others: that He may try you in the gifts He hath given you: for thy Lord is quick in punishment: yet He is indeed Oft-forgiving, Most Merciful." (Quran 6:165)

"That which is on earth we have made but as a glittering show for the earth, in order that We may test them - as to which of them are best in conduct." (Quran 18:7)

Some righteous do receive rewards in this life, though unlike the Bible, it is clarified that the reward in heaven will be more:

"And Allah gave them a reward in this world, and the excellent reward of the Hereafter. For Allah Loveth those who do good." (Quran 3:148)

Therefore, unlike the Bible, it is explained plainly that some righteous people are rewarded in both lives, and the Quran does not make the mistake in saying the righteous will be rewarded more on earth. Instead, the Better reward is in the Heaven.

202. Death in Hell?

Errancy; The Bible claims that the sinners will be destroyed;

"And death and hell were cast into the lake of fire. This is the second death." (Revelation 20:14, 2 Thessalonians 1:9) while in contradiction, the Bible says elsewhere's that the sinners will live a torturous life;

"And in hell he lift up his eyes, being in torments, and seeth Abraham afar off, and Lazarus in his bosom. And he cried and said, Father Abraham, have mercy on me, and send Lazarus, that he may dip the tip of his finger in water, and cool my tongue; for I am tormented in this flame." (Luke 16: 23-24)

Excuse; That is what it says but that is not what it means. Death in (Revelation 20:14) is not a physical one but maybe a spiritual one like Adam experienced from the garden of Eden.

Rebuttal: (See Reply letter [E] in Rebuttal Chart). Because the Bible does not speak about skin regeneration as in the Quran, we have to

199

logically and scientifically take the word 'death' literally. Any human body (being thrown and trapped in fire), dies in Hell, as the Bible conflictingly says.

Correction: The Holy Quran clarifies that our skin will be regenerated in Hell; hence, we will be kept conscience to feel the fire:

"Lo! Those who disbelieve Our revelations, We shall expose them to the Fire. As often as their skins are consumed We shall exchange them for fresh skins that they may taste the torment. Lo! Allah is ever Mighty, Wise." (Quran 4:56)

"He who will be flung to the great fire Wherein he will neither die nor live." (Quran 87:12-13)

203. Feeling the Fire?

Errancy; Does burned Skin Feel? According to the Bible, the sinners will be tormented in Hell's fire;

"And in hell he lifts up his eyes, being in torments, and seeth Abraham afar off, and Lazarus in his bosom. And he cried and said, Father Abraham, have mercy on me, and send Lazarus, that he may dip the tip of his finger in water, and cool my tongue; for I am tormented in this flame." (Luke 16: 23-24)

And

"Depart from me, ye cursed, into everlasting fire, prepared for the devil and his angels" (Matthew 25:41)

Yet according to doctors, burned skin no longer has the ability to feel because of the damaged nerve endings. The skin becomes hard and even burns off our body like charcoaled piece of meat. Therefore, the notion that we will continue to feel pain in hell according to the Bible is unexplainable and scientifically incorrect.

Excuse; None available.

Correction: Quran teaches the skin is regenerated:

"Lo! Those who disbelieve Our revelations, We shall expose them to the Fire. As often as their skins are consumed We shall exchange them for fresh skins that they may taste the torment. Lo! Allah is ever Mighty, Wise." (Quran 4:56)

204. Earth Forever?

Errancy; "A generation goes, and a generation comes, but the earth remains forever." (Ecclesiastes 1:4, Psalms 78:69, 104:5) *Vs* "Heaven and earth will pass away, but my words will not pass away." (Luke 21:33, 2 Peter 3:10).

Excuse; Mistranslation. The word "forever" should actually be "long time".

Rebuttal: (See Reply letter [I] in Rebuttal Chart). Again Christians trying to re-invent word meanings to avoid one of hundreds of contradictions.

Correction: The Holy Quran confirms that the earth will not last forever; instead, there will be a day when the earth is destroyed:

"And when the earth is spread out And hath cast out all that was in her, and is empty" (Quran 84:3-4)

205. Heaven Eternal?

Errancy; Believers will inherit eternal life in heaven. (1 Peter 1:4) *Vs* Heaven will pass away. (Psalms 102:25-26, Luke 21:33, 2 Peter 3:10)

Excuse; Mistranslation.

Rebuttal: (See Reply letter [I] in Rebuttal Chart)

Correction: The Holy Quran, unlike the Bible, explains there are different levels of heaven;

"He Who created the seven heavens one above another; No want of proportion wilt thou see in the Creation of (Allah) Most Gracious. So turn thy vision again: seest thou any flaw?" (Quran 67:3)

Therefore, when the first is destroyed, there are upper levels for the righteous. The earthly level will indeed collapse at the Day of Judgment;

"A day when the heaven with the clouds will be rent asunder and the angels will be sent down, a grand descent." (Quran 25:25)

206. Feeling Tempted?

Errancy; Christians claim that God needed to send Jesus to earth to know the temptations of the flesh in order to defeat it;

"Jesus returned from the Jordan full of the Holy Spirit and was led by the Spirit into the desert, where he was tempted by the Devil for forty days." (Luke 4:1-2)

"For what the law could not do, in that it was weak through the flesh, God sending his own Son in the likeness of sinful flesh, and for sin, condemned sin in the flesh" (Romans 8:3)

Excuse; None available.

Correction: Allah is already the omnipresent, God did not need to send anyone to learn about your temptations.

Allah does not need to come down because He is already aware of everything that goes on everything and does not need to descend from the Heaven to see anything for He can already see it:

"It was We Who created man, and We know what dark suggestions his soul makes to him: for We are nearer to him than (his) jugular vein." (Quran 50:16)

207. Who Stole?

Errancy; Christians claim that Jesus is God, and while Jesus was surrounded by a crowd, someone stole some power from Jesus;

"And a woman who had had a flow of blood for twelve years and could not be healed by any one, came up behind him, and touched the fringe of his garment; and immediately her flow of blood ceased. And Jesus said, "Who was it that touched me?" When all denied it, Peter said, "Master, the multitudes surround you and press upon you!" But Jesus said, "Some one touched me; for I perceive that power has gone forth from me." (Luke 8:43:46)

Excuse; None available.

Correction: God in the Quran has full knowledge and awareness of what is or is not taken:

"Allah indeed knows those who steal away from among you, concealing themselves; therefore let those beware who go against his order lest a trial afflict them, or a grievous penalty be inflicted on them." (Quran 24:63)

208. All Sins Equal?

Errancy; Christians claim that all sins have an equal consequence, thus there is no difference between modesty or murder;

"For whoever keeps the whole law but fails in one point has become guilty of all of it." (James 2:10)

Vs.

"Two men owed money to a certain moneylender. One owed him five hundred denarii, and the other fifty. Neither of them had the money to pay him back, so he canceled the debts of both. Now which of them will love him more?" Simon replied, "I suppose the one who had the bigger debt canceled." "You have judged correctly," Jesus said. (Luke 7:41-43)

The "debt" refers to a person's sin against God. There are many references in both the Old and New Testament on how various sins will be punished differently, proving that not all sins are equal. Some sins push us further away from God than others.

Excuse; None available.

Correction: God in the Quran is a fair Judge who confronts us on a system of accountability, where every decimal of bad or good we do is taken into consideration for a verdict:

"On that Day will men proceed in companies sorted out, to be shown the deeds that they (had done). Then shall anyone who has done an atom's weight of good, see it! And anyone who has done an atom's weight of evil, shall see it. (Quran 99:6-8)

209. Jews Unconditionally Chosen?

Errancy; The Bible talks about the Jews as humans picked by God above all other humans and regardless of what they do, they are unconditionally chosen above all by God;

"For thou art an holy people unto the Lord thy God: the Lord thy God hath chosen thee to be a special people unto himself, above all people that are upon the face of the earth. The Lord did not set his love upon you, nor choose you, because ye were more in number than any people; for ye were the fewest of all people" (Deuteronomy 7:6-7)

God in the Bible did not choose Jews because they were sinless;

"Understand therefore, that the LORD thy God giveth thee not this good land to possess it for thy righteousness; for thou art a stubborn people." (Deuteronomy 9:6)

Instead, the Bible says that all Jews are unconditionally chosen above all other humans because of a promise made to their forefathers;

"But because the LORD loved you, and because he would keep the oath which he had sworn unto your fathers, hath the LORD brought you out with a mighty hand, and redeemed you out of the house of bondmen, from the hand of Pharaoh king of Egypt." (Deuteronomy 7:8)

Vs.

"Do you Israelites think you are more important to me than the Ethiopians ?" asks the LORD. "I brought you out of Egypt, but have I not done as much for other nations, too? I brought the Philistines from Crete and led the Arameans out of Kir" Amos 9:7

Excuse; None available.

Correction: God states in the Quran that the favor towards Jews was conditional:

"And We gave (Clear) Warning to the Children of Israel in the Book, that twice would they do mischief on the earth and be elated with mighty arrogance (and twice would they be punished)! It may be that your Lord may (yet) show Mercy unto you; but if ye revert (to your sins), We shall revert (to Our punishments): And we have made Hell a prison for those who reject (all Faith). (Quran 17:4-8)

The Quran explains, it is not who you are, it is what you do that grants you favor with God, you are chosen for your belief, not your ethnicity:

"And there are, certainly, among the People of the Book (Jews and Christians), those who believe in Allah, and that which has been revealed to you and in that which has been revealed to them, humbling themselves before Allah: They will not sell the Revelations of Allah for a miserable gain! For them is a reward with their Lord, and Allah is swift in account." (Quran 3:199)

210. <u>Unconditional Love?</u>

Errancy; The Bible teaches that God will love the sinners (Matthew 5:43-45, Romans 5:6 – 10, 8:38–39) *Vs.* God will not love the sinners (Hosea 9:15);

"I hated them: for the wickedness of their doings I will drive them out of mine house, I will love them no more: all their princes are revolters."

Excuse; None available.

Correction: It would be a punishment on the Righteous if God loved the sinners, because then the Judgment of God would have no equitable value, and Heaven would be intertwined evil murderers along with their victims, making the potential of more violence and revenge in the Afterlife. Instead, God in the Quran is a fair Judge and gives love to those who do not reject the love of God:

"That He may reward those who believe and work righteous deeds, out of his Bounty. For He loves not those who reject Faith." (Quran 30:45)

Conclusion

In the manner of Moses leading Jews out of Egypt, the Quran has also parted a sea of errors in the Bible to lead humans to Heaven. We come to several conclusions at the end of this monumental exploration. We have found that what thousands of Bible editors could not do for thousands of years, the Quran has produced in a precise and clear method.

Another finding from our research is that the Holy Quran brings an acceptable balance between the Jews and Christians. For Jews, Jesus is turned from a carpenter to a Messiah, for Christians, Jesus is turned from a God to a Prophet, and the balance is made so that both Jews and Christians can accept each other and have a shared and plausible belief in Jesus and his Creator.

For Jews, Salvation was made easier, for Christians, Salvation was made harder, again giving a level of balance that both sides can agree on and accept. In addition, a clearer explanation was made of the fate of earth and the Afterlife. In both Judaism and Christianity, the Rabbis and Priests are stripped of their powers to reinterpret scriptures that caused humans to deviate from the path of God.

The pinnacle of unity that the Quran brings between Jews and Christians is the fate of Jesus. Christ is not used as a scapegoat in the Quran; there was no need for Jesus to die to achieve salvation as in Christianity. The Quran explicitly says the Jews did not kill Jesus, which was the fuel for many crusades and even the Holocaust according to many historians.

In Adolph Hitler's autobiography *Mein Kampf*, it's repeatedly proclaimed he was doing the "Lord's work." At a Christmas celebration in 1926, Hitler stated; "Christ was the greatest early fighter in the battle against the world enemy, the Jews ... The work that Christ started but could not finish, I -- Adolph Hitler -- will conclude."

Much of the Nazi propaganda labeled Jews as "Christ killers", it is my sincere belief that if Hitler and many of the persecutors of Jews, believed that Jews did not kill Jesus as the Quran teaches, then millions of lives would have been saved. In fact, during many of the crusades and the Holocaust, Muslim nations, who saw Jews as fellow monotheists who did not kill Jesus, sheltered and protected Jews from the chasing crusaders. The Quran arbitrates between Jews and Christians to unite them as brotherly and sisterly Muslims.

CONCLUSION

Another conclusion is that the Quran empowers women in both Judaism and Christianity with freedom of speech, inheritance rights, and marriage rights unavailable from the Bible. The Quran removes the curse and gender guilt blamed on Eve and her female descendants.

Modern technology has and will increase the already fastest growing religion in the world simply because the internet and powerful search engines are allowing people to discover how Islam towers in truth above other religions in a magnitude unfathomed before.

The deeper we are able to look inside texts, pin pointing words and phrases for comparison, the more we are able to discover the Divine nature of the Quran. This is even more proof that in the days of Prophet Muhammad (peace be upon him), where computers were over a millennium away, it would have been impossible for a human to make the corrections because today it is taking extensive computer assisted researching just to realize that these corrections exist. For example, modern surgeons use endoscopes to search deep inside passages just as computers as used by authors to search deep inside passages, both discovering the works by God and detailed information unavailable to humans prior to these powerful searching tools.

We have also managed to dispel many myths by completing this massive manuscript. We have manifested how the Quran mends, rather than mimics the Bible. Furthermore, we have established that the Quran is not from Satan as some anti-Islamic preachers claim. In fact, by Islam re-confirming the validity of the laws in the Bible, the Quran actually exposes an attempt by Satan to lead people away from God. Satan from the start (with Adam and Eve), tried to get humans not to obey God, as Satan tricked humans with a brown tree and red apple, it was done again with a brown cross and red blood. Meaning most Christians have been led to assume that they are no longer responsible for obeying the laws of God, claiming the blood of Jesus on the crucifix atoned all their sins and made them closer to God. This is exactly the same type of manipulation Satan maneuvered on Adam and Eve; Satan told Adam and Eve if they accept the red apple on the brown tree, they too would become more God like. The sinister constant in both scenarios is; taking shortcuts that outcome in disobeying God. In the Quran, this salvation shortcut that people are tempted with in the Gospel is removed, instead we are taught as in Judaism, that everyone is responsible for their own sins, thus keeping the laws as well as faith in God are both the keys to salvation, rather than just one or the other.

There are many more miracles in the Quran including scientific, mathematical, and literary astonishments. Consequently, the Quran not only stands on its own, but also rescues the Bible. In closing, while there are over 200 valid corrections, if the reader reluctantly accepts only one way the Qur'an corrects the Bible, then the reader must realize it is a blessing and not an attack on the Bible. The Quran helps the reader believe the stories in the Bible. Thus, Islam is the world's fastest growing religion simply because truth prevails. At the time of Prophet Muhammad (peace be upon him), the ratio of Muslims compared to Jews and Christians were; one Muslim for every million Jews and Christians. Today the ratio is, one Jew for every 100 Muslims, and the ratio gap between Muslims and Christians has dissipated down to 1 Muslim for every 2 Christians. According to "The Almanac Book of Facts", the population increased 137% within the past decade, Christianity increased 46%, while Islam increased 235%.

We invite the non-Muslim readers to accept Islam (submission to God) as taught in the Holy Quran. We leave you with a translation of an invitation letter to Islam from Prophet Muhammad (peace be upon him) to the former non-Muslim Kings of the Middle East:

"Praise be to Allah, the King, the All-Holy, the Peacemaker, the Keeper of Faith, the Watcher. He is Allah, there is no divinity but He, the Sovereign Lord, the Holy One, the All-peaceable, the Keeper of Faith, the Guardian, the Majestic, the Compeller, the All-sublime. Glorified be Allah from all that they associate with Him. And I testify that Jesus, son of Mary, is the spirit of Allah and His Word which He cast to Mary the Virgin, the good, the pure, so that she conceived Jesus. Allah created him from His Spirit and His Breath as He created Adam by His Hand and His Breath. I call you to Allah, the Unique, without partner, to His obedience, and to follow me and to believe in that which came to me, for I am the Messenger of Allah. Peace be upon all those who follow true guidance."

May God bless you with the hunger for knowledge and the ability to accept the truth once the knowledge has come to you.

We also invite the Muslims to fulfill your duties in inviting non-Muslims to Islam. In the same endeavor that this research has been made for the non-Muslims, we made this book equally for the Muslims. We pray that the Muslims have found this book confidence building and has given Muslims the optimism to invite non-Muslims.

CONCLUSION

Dozens of Bible Universities offer an increasingly popular degree in trying to solve Bible issues. Instead of these young men and women spending years of their lives to become apologetics, we encourage you the reader, to invite these college students and even their professors to discover the corrections in the Quran.

In my own public and private comparative religion debates with Jews and Christians, I have found this richly loaded compilation very useful and easily used as a topical encyclopedic [rebuttal and answer] stockpile. Any one of the ways the Quran corrects the Bible in this book are a point of dialog on the similarities and superiority of the Quran. The beginning and ending of the debate between you the Muslim and the non-Muslim are already mapped out for you here, to prepare you and give you the instrument to effectively show the Light and Love of God in the Quran to the non-Muslim. We are commanded over seventeen times in the Holy Quran specifically to invite the people of the Book (Jews and Christians), to the path of Allah. For example:

"Say: O People of the Book! Come to an agreement between us and you: that we shall worship none but Allah, and that we shall ascribe no partner unto Him, and that none of us shall take others for lords beside Allah. And if they turn away, then say: Bear witness that we are they who have surrendered (unto Him)." (Quran 3:64)

Besides inviting Christians, we must increase our efforts 100% to invite the Jews. Muslims inviting Jews to Islam is very rare. God gave us the Quran to share with both the Jews and Christians. Prophet Muhammad (peace and blessings upon him) teaching us by example, himself invited Jews to Islam and also sent Muslims to convert Jews, and promised they will be greatly Blessed. In conclusion, our disobedience, pessimism and lack of confidence towards inviting Jews to Islam has resulted in Israel being the only non-Muslim country in the Middle East.

The Trinitarian Christian group "Jews for Jesus" has converted 300,000 Jews. The Jews endured the Crusades and Holocaust at the hands of the Christians, and Christianity teaches that the Laws of Moses are like rags to be done away with, yet nearly half a million Jews accepted Christianity just by the Christians asking them to. So fulfill your duty and simply ask in a polite manner as we're commanded to:

"Invite (all) to the Way of thy Lord with wisdom and beautiful preaching; and argue with them in ways that are best and most gracious: for thy Lord knoweth best, who have strayed from His Path, and who receive guidance." (Quran 16:125)

Bibliography

Abdullah, Yusuf Ali. *The Holy Qur'an, English Translation of the Meanings and Commentary*. Madinah, Saudi Arabia: King Fahd Holy Qur'an Printing Complex, 1991.

Abou Shabanah, Mirvet. *A Favourable Aspect of the Quran in Honouring the Woman*. Cairo, Egypt: The Supreme Council of Islamic Affairs, 1999.

Ahmed, Mansur and Saifullah, Muhammad and Ghoniem, Muhammad. *Refutation Of The Borrowing Theories Of The Qur'an. English.* http://www.islamicawareness.org/Quran/Sources/:Oct. 20, 2003.

Ajijola, AlHaj A.D. *The Myth of the Cross*. Lahore, Pakistan: Islamic Publications Limited, 1975.

Al Fandy, Muhammad Jamaluddin. *On Cosmic Verses in the Quran*. Cairo Egypt: Supreme Council for Islamic Affairs, 1994.

Ali, Maulana Muhammad. *History of the Prophets as Narrated in the Holy Quran Compared with the Bible*. Columbus, OH: Ahmadiyya Anjuman Isha'at Islam Lahore, Inc, 1996.

Archer, Gleason L. *New International Encyclopedia of Bible Difficulties*. Grand Rapids, Michigan: Zondervan, 1982.

Bucaille, Maurice. *The Bible, the Quran, and Science*. Indianapolis, IN: American Trust Publications, 1979.

Burr, William Henry. *Self-Contradictions of the Bible*. New York, NY: A. J. Davis and Company, 1860.

Clarke, Adam and Earle, Ralph H. *Adam Clarke's Commentary on the Bible*. Nashville, TN: World Bible Publishing, 1996.

Deedat, Ahmed. *Was Jesus Crucified?* Chicago, IL: Kazi Publications, 1992.

Dirks, Jerald F. *The Cross and The Crescent*. Beltsville, MD: Amana Publications, 2003.

Fatoohi, Louay and Al Dargazelli, Shetha. *History Testifies to the Infallibility of the Quran*. Kuala Lumpur: A.S. Noordeen, 2001.

Geiger, Abraham. *Judaism and Islam.* New York, NY: KTAV Publishing House, Inc., 1970.

Geisler, Norman and Howe, Thomas. *When Critics Ask.* Grand Rapids, MI: Baker Books, 1992.

Geisler, Norman and Saleeb, Abdul. *Answering Islam; The Crescent in Light of the Cross.* 2nd ed. Grand Rapids, MI: Baker Book House, 2002.

Geisler, Norman L. and Brooks, Ronald M. *When Skeptics Ask.* Wheaton, Ill: Victor Books, 1990.

Geisler, Norman L. and Mackenzie, Ralph E. *Roman Catholics and Evangelicals; Agreements and Differences.* Grand Rapids, MI: Baker Book House, 1995.

Geisler, Norman L. and Rhodes, Ron. *When Cultists Ask.* Grand Rapids, MI: Baker Book House, 1997.

Ghounem, Mohamed. *Who Is Our Savior? Allah or Jesus.* Cairo Egypt: M.G. Enterprise, 2000.

Haley, John W. *Alleged Discrepancies of the Bible.* Grand Rapids, MI: Baker Book House, 1996.

Henry, Matthew. *Matthew Henry's Commentary on the Whole Bible.* Peabody, MA : Hendrickson Publishers, Inc, 1991.

Ibn Abdullah, Misha'al. *What Did Jesus Really Say?* Ann Arbor, MI: IANA, 1996.

Jamieson, Robert and Fausset, A. R. and Brown, David. *Jamieson-Fausset-Brown Bible Commentary.* Peabody, MA: Hendrickson Publishers, Inc., 1997.

Kaiser, Walter C. and Davids, Peter H. *Hard Sayings of the Bible.* Downers Grove, IL: InterVarsity Press, 1992.

Katz, Jochen. *Jesus and the 99 Names.* English. http://answering-islam.org/Who/99names.html:October 21, 2003.

McKinsey, C. Dennis. *The Encyclopedia of Biblical Errancy.* Del Mar, CA: Promethean Books, 1995.

Nave, Orville J. *Nave's Topical Bible*. Peabody, MA: Hendrickson Publishers, 2002.

Neusner, Jacob and Sonn, Tamara. *Comparing Religions through Law: Judaism and Islam*. New York, NY: Routledge, 1999.

Pickthall, Marmaduke William, and Arafat Kamil Ashshi. *The Meaning of the Glorious Quran: Text and Explanatory Translation*. Beltsville, MD: Amana Publications, 1994.

Richards, Larry. *735 Baffling Bible Questions Answered*. Grand Rapids, MI: Fleming H. Revell, 1997.

Shakir, Mahomodali. *The Quran Translation*. Elmhurst, NY: Tahrike Tarsile Quran, 1986.

Smith, Ben J. *Differences; The Bible and the Koran*. Nashville, TN: Cumberland House Publishing, Inc., 2002.

Strong, James H. *Strong's Exhaustive Concordance*. Grand Rapids, MI: Baker Book House, 1989.

The Bible, King James Version. Oak Harbor, WA: Logos Research Systems, Inc., 1995.

The Good News Translation. Grand Rapids, MI: Zondervan, 2001.

Torrey, Charles Cutler. *The Jewish Foundation of Islam*. New York, NY: Jewish Institute of Religion Press, 1933.

Torrey, R. A. *Torrey's New Topical Textbook*. Murfreesboro, TN: Sword of the Lord Publishers, 2000.

Wells, Steve. *Skeptic's Annotated Bible*. English. http://www.skepticsannotatedbible.com/:Oct 14, 2003.

Index

Aaron, 31, 33, 34, 35, 71, 72, 73, 74, 89, 116

Adam, 36, 44, 45, 62, 82, 85, 86, 104, 105, 106, 107, 119, 120, 123, 134, 142, 151, 164, 185, 190, 199, 210

adultery, 34, 83, 96, 97, 108, 109, 110, 112, 115, 116, 143

angels, 18, 23, 27, 48, 49, 100, 101, 104, 136, 143, 146, 148, 149, 151, 158, 164, 165, 166, 189, 190, 200, 201

Animals, 43, 54

apostates, 70, 71, 197

Babylon, 86, 87, 88, 145

blood, 62, 70, 113, 148, 153, 158, 159, 160, 187, 193

bribery, 69

Cain, 36

Catholics, 117, 151, 211

celibacy, 58

crucifixion, 45, 125, 126, 127, 128, 130, 138, 141, 175

curse, 28, 46, 52, 53, 60, 63, 64, 65, 87, 88, 102, 176, 177, 192

David, 34, 35, 75, 98, 99, 145, 170, 211

death, 31, 32, 44, 45, 46, 47, 53, 59, 60, 61, 70, 71, 79, 81, 83, 85, 86, 100, 109, 110, 115, 119, 121, 128, 129, 132, 137, 140, 144, 147, 149, 150, 164, 166, 173, 180, 181, 182, 188, 194, 198, 199, 200

divorce, 83, 96, 97, 109, 110, 112, 114, 122

earth, 14, 17, 18, 19, 20, 21, 22, 24, 26, 27, 28, 29, 32, 35, 37, 41, 42, 44, 46, 47, 48, 49, 50, 51, 53, 58, 65, 75, 76, 80, 86, 88, 99, 102, 104, 117, 118, 121, 139, 147, 148, 151, 153, 154, 157, 158, 159, 160, 163, 164, 165, 166,

167, 176, 177, 181, 183, 186, 191, 192, 193, 194, 198, 199, 201

embryology, 54, 55

fear, 22, 37, 70, 76, 78, 84, 86, 99, 102, 110, 120, 131, 139, 173, 179, 180, 187, 192

flood, 28, 88

Goliath, 98, 99

Halal, 59

heaven, 17, 18, 29, 42, 43, 48, 50, 51, 65, 66, 70, 76, 80, 90, 101, 138, 139, 145, 151, 154, 156, 158, 164, 165, 182, 183, 184, 186, 189, 191, 195, 196, 198, 199, 201

hell, 77, 133, 149, 166, 179, 190, 195, 199, 200

Interest, 68

Iron, 24

Isaac, 35, 52, 95, 96, 97, 98

Ishmael, 35, 92, 93, 95, 96, 97, 98

Israel, 23, 31, 32, 33, 34, 36, 37, 48, 60, 80, 82, 99, 101, 102, 103, 115, 125, 126, 131, 147, 152, 156, 172, 176, 177, 192

Jesus, 4, 13, 17, 21, 22, 31, 35, 36, 38, 39, 45, 52, 63, 64, 65, 66, 67, 75, 76, 77, 80, 83, 85, 86, 90, 102, 107, 109, 110, 112, 113, 115, 116, 119, 120, 124, 125, 126, 127, 128, 129, 130, 131, 132, 133, 134, 135, 136, 137, 138, 139, 140, 141, 142, 143, 144, 145, 146, 147, 148, 149, 150, 151, 152, 153, 154, 155, 156, 157, 158, 159, 160, 161, 162, 163, 164, 165, 166, 167, 168, 169, 170, 171, 172, 173, 174, 175, 176, 177, 178, 179, 180, 181, 182, 183, 184, 185, 186, 188, 190, 191, 192, 194, 196, 198, 210, 211

213

Printed in the United Kingdom
by Lightning Source UK Ltd.
108201UKS00001B/151-159